Edition No. 1

ISBN-13: 978-0615664750
(Catmoon Media)
ISBN-10: 061566475X

For more information or comments contact Catmoon Media at:
catmoon-media@mindspring.com.

GRAVE WORDS

Epitaphs of South Carolina

By Craig Metts

Published by Catmoon Media
Columbia, South Carolina

*To Colleen for your
Peace, Love, Understanding,
and Patience While Visiting
Thousands of Graves….*

TABLE OF CONTENTS:

INTRODUCTION:

The inevitability of the end of our own brief existence is, most certainly, the impetus for the often amazing practice of death and burial. Ancient people simply buried their dead and heaped a mound of stones to mark the grave. As language, writing and the worship of gods emerged the practice of the burial procedure changed. The first burial grounds were called Necropolei (Cities of the Dead) and became common place in the Roman world with grave marked by upright slabs of stone called stelai. These stones were decorated with sculpture, urns, and marble vases and were at first simple in design. The stelai became more ornate and as the written language developed so did the practice of inscribing the tomb with an epitaph.

One of the most famous of these early epitaphs is known as the tomb of the *Happy Man* and reads:

SPRINKLE MY ASHES WITH GOOD WINES

AND WITH PERFUMED OIL OF SPIKENARD;

STRANGER, ADD BALSAM AND CRIMSON ROSES.

EVER, WITHOUT TEARS, MY URN KNOWS SPRING,

FOR I HAVE NOT DIED.

I HAVE CHANGED MY STATE.

These early burial stelai with their symbols and style of epitaphs were the beginning of our modern style of the burial procedure. During the Middle Ages the practice of placing an effigy on the tomb of the nobility, rich and pious became commonplace, as well as the use of glass encasements, so that the mourners could view and remember the ones that had passed away. The tombs of the noble and wealthy were often placed within the church sanctuary, while those of lesser status were buried in the church yards of England and Europe's great cathedrals. Other forms of burial took place on one's own property, while the poor were often buried in unmarked graves.

Burial grounds were eventually established in and around urban areas and were called cemeteries, which mean "Sleeping Place." The first concept of the modern cemetery in the New World was created in plans dating 1725, that established a burial ground outside of the City of New Orleans, in early America. The reasons were that the city was becoming overcrowded and a fear that bodies buried in the churchyards would soon contaminate the already high water levels.

South Carolina was no exception and followed the same patterns as the rest of America in the care for its dead. There are many fine examples of early family

7

graveyards, church burial grounds and huge planned and manicured cemeteries across the State. The typical styles and protocol for burial and grave markers also reflect the same characteristics of the rest of America. Early markers were simply field stones or wooden crosses, but eventually carved stone markers, mostly made of dark gray slate, were used to mark the dead. Early epitaphs and gravestone art usually imitated English styles that were blunt and descriptive. Common symbols that appear on the earliest of grave markers are the "winged figure of death" and the "skull and crossbones." Other early American symbols include figs, representing fertility and the hourglass, to symbolize man's brevity on earth. Slowly, the "winged death" gave way to Victorian styled angels and cupids.

The use of dark slate appears to be common until the Victorian Age until it was abandoned for white marble. Even the epitaphs themselves became more kind and gentle with phrases such as "gone away", "at rest" and "asleep." Victorian gravestone art marks the zenith of burial monuments, with intricate hand carved works of art created from white marble, granite, and even alabaster and other exotic materials. However, perhaps due to the Industrial Revolution, the two World Wars of the early Twentieth Century, gravestone art seems to have disappeared and given way to smaller and less obtrusive headstones.

Sadly, even though modern headstones are more affordable and make the maintenance of cemetery grounds simpler, the decline of personal epitaphs and cemetery art extinguishes an age-old tradition of celebrating the passing of our deceased into the next world. Epitaphs, as well as cemetery art, offer the living a very unique vision of who our ancestors were, not just from a genealogical standpoint, but from an artistic and cultural one as well. Each grave and epitaph can tell a story that is as unique as the person buried there along with a great wealth of information that is written in stone. One need only visit a few of the thousands of cemeteries and churches across South Carolina to realize the truly fascinating epitaphs and great works of art that exist under the sun.

While not an exhaustive listing of epitaphs, the following is a survey of the curious and beautiful inscriptions that exist in stone across the State. This is an attempt to entertain and reveal a treasure that should be cherished and carefully preserved. It is a measure to reveal a lost art and identify typical characteristics of epitaphs and remembrances of the deceased. For this reason, it is hoped that the following will inspire those to preserve, and perhaps even rekindle, the ancient art of remembrance and celebration for the dead.

NOTE TO THE READER:

HERE LIES...... over a decade of research in libraries, record halls, and field collection that involved the reconstruction of headstones, grave rubbings and dustings to reveal weathered inscriptions. Over a thousand unique epitaphs were collected from hundreds of locations across the State. Every effort was made to transcribe each epitaph and inscription, verbatim and in its entirety. I have selected the most interesting to be included in this book and categorize them; footnoted if needed, and included interesting stories and information about those interred.

As one can only imagine, the style, font, punctuation, grammar and spelling vary greatly from inscription to inscription. Therefore, I have made no corrections or edits to the transcriptions, and as a protocol, capitalized the epitaphs using the same font and format for the sake of consistency and ease of reading. Finally, each inscription is given a unique code in parenthesis. The first two letters represent the county from where the epitaphs were collected and at the end of this book is a county index based upon this code.

CHAPTER 1
EXTRAORDINARY PLACES

Here lies One Whose Name was writ in Water

Epitaph John Keats

THE JOURNEY OF AGNES OF GLASGOW

Agnes of Glasgow is the subject of an early American legend. She followed her lover, British Officer Lt. Angus McPherson, to America during the Revolutionary War by stowing away on a ship on its way to Charleston, SC. Agnes soon heard McPherson was (or would soon be) assigned to his post in Camden, SC and may have possibly been wounded in an earlier action.

Without means, money or map she traveled through the wilderness hoping to find him and along the way, she befriended a Wateree Indian who helped her reach Camden. Exhausted, sick and heartbroken she couldn't find McPherson and soon died. She was buried in the Old Quaker Cemetery in Camden. Legend has it McPherson arrived shortly thereafter and learned of her journey and death. Her ghost is said to still haunt the Old Quaker Cemetery, looking for her lover. Her epitaph is below.

HERE LIES
THE BODY
OF AGNES OF
GLASGOW
WHO DEPARTED THIS LIFE
FEBRUARY 12, 1780, AGE 20
(KS-3)

HALL'S GREAT HALLS

Ainsley Hall was a wealthy merchant who lived in Columbia, at what is now known as the Hampton-Preston Mansion (later purchased by Revolutionary General Wade Hampton in 1823). In 1818 he commissioned influential architect Robert Mills (designer of the Washington Monument) to build a second palatial estate, now known as the Robert Mills House. Both homes are some of the few to survive the burning of Columbia by General Sherman and his men during the Civil War. His epitaph reads:

AINSLEY HALL
WAS BORN AT
BAMBOUGH CASTLE,
NORTHUMBERLAND,
ENGLAND
ON THE 4th JULY
1783;
AND DIED AT THE BOTETOURT SPRINGS
VIRGINIA
ON THE 18th AUGUST
1823;
HIS REMAINS
HAVE BEEN BROUGHT HITHER,
AND THIS MONUMENT ERECTED
BY HIS
BEREAVED WIDOW
(RC-31)

HUGUENOTS IN SOUTH CAROLINA

There were many reasons why people traveled thousands of miles to settle in early America. Some were driven by profit or for military reasons, and others, to escape religious persecution and practice their beliefs openly. One such group was the Huguenots, or French Calvinist. They came to the American Colonies after the Edict of Nantes (granting rights to French Protestants) was revoked by Louis XIV in 1685.

Charleston was home to a sizable Huguenot community with its own church and burial ground. Below is the epitaph of Henry Bounetheau, a well-known miniature portrait painter whose subjects included many heroes of the Revolution and leaders of early America.

His motto, "Un Dieu Un Roi", translates as "One God, One King" a very Protestant statement meaning "God is the Only King".

HENRY BREINTUAL BOUNETHEAU
DEC. 14, 1797 – JANY 31, 1877
SON OF PETER BOUNETHEAU
AND GRANDSON OF JOHN BOUNETHEAU
WHO CAME TO CHARLESTON FROM
LaROCHELLE FRANCE
ON THE REVOCATION OF THE EDICT OF NANTES 1685
THE LAST TWO ARE INTERRED BENEATH THIS CHURCH
UN DIEU UN ROI
(CT-50)

Front side:

PATRICK CALHOUN
THE FATHER OF
CATHERINE, WILLIAM, JAMES,
JOHN CALWELL & PATRICK
CALHOUN
BORN IN THE COUNTY OF DONEGAL
IRELAND JUNE 11, 1727
AND DIED JANUARY 15th 1796
IN THE 69th YEAR.

Right side:

MARTHA CALWELL
THE WIFE OF PATRICK CALHOUN
AND THE MOTHER OF
CATHERINE, WILLIAM, JAMES,
JOHN CALWELL & PATRICK
CALHOUN
BORN ON CUB CREEK,
CHARLOTTE COUNTY VIRGINIA 1750
DIED IN MAY 1802
AGED 52 YEARS.

Left side:

CATHERINE
THE DAUGHTER OF
PATRICK & MARTHA CALHOUN.
AND THE FIRST WIFE
OF THE REVEREND DOCTOR WADDEL
DIED IN MARCH 1796
IN THE 21st YEAR OF HER AGE
WITHOUT ISSUE.

Back side:

ERECTED BY
JOHN CALWELL CALHOUN.
THE SURVIVING MEMBER OF
THE FAMILY, 1844.
(AB-16)

HERE LIES INTERRED
IN HOPE
OF JOYFUL RESURRECTION
THE REMAINS OF
MR. JAMES LEGG BRICKLAYER
A NATIVE OF THE
ISLE OF WRIGHT, ENGLAND
AND TOWN OF GATCOMB,
& A RESIDENT OF THIS CITY FOR TWENTY ONE YEARS
HE DEPARTED THIS LIFE ON THE 7TH DAY OF MARCH
1805
IN THE 43RD YEAR OF HIS AGE
HERE LIES PROUD RATIONALS! A BROTHER'S SHADE!
ONCE ON EARTH! NOW THE PROPERTY OF WORMS!
BEING OF YESTERDAY AND NO TOMORROW!
WHO LIV'D IN TERRORS, AND IN PANGS EXPIRED!
(CT-77)

HERE REST
THE REMAINS OF
*CAPT. JOHN HERBERT DENT
OF THE U.S. NAVY
A NATIVE OF MARYLAND
WHO WAS BORN ON THE 22nd FEB. 1782
AND DIED ON THE 29th JULY 1823
AT HIS PLANTATION IN
ST. BARTHOLOMEW'S PARISH
GREATLY BELOVED AND
LAMENTED BY
HIS FAMILY.
(CL-2)

*Captain Dent was the acting Captain on the frigate Constitution in the 1804 War with Tripoli and War of 1812.

17

"HERE LIE THE REMAINS"
OF THE
HONBLE ROBERT DANIELL
A BRAVE MAN WHO HAD LONG SERVED
KING WILLIAM IN HIS WARS BOTH LAND AND SEA.
AND AFTERWARDS GOVERNED THIS PROVINCE
UNDER THE LORD PROPRIETORS.
HE DIED ON THE FIRST DAY OF MAY
IN THE YEAR 1718
AGED 72 YEARS
(CT-44)

SACRED
TO THE
MEMORY OF
CAPTN. JAMES BERRY
WHO DEPARTED THIS LIFE
IN CAMDEN NOV. 29th 1813
AGED 22 YEARS
A CITIZEN OF YORK DISTRICT
MY FRIENDS AND NEIGHBOURS IF YOU CALL
TO SEE WHERE I DO LIE
REMEMBER WELL THAT YOU'R FROM HOME
AND MIGHT DIE AS WELL AS I.
(KS-6)

DR. JOHN LYNCH
BORN ON THE ATLANTIC OCEAN
8, JANUARY, 1819
DIED COLUMBIA, S. C.
20, OCT. 1881
(RC-44)

JOHN S. PRESTON
BORN AT THE SALT WORKS NEAR
ABINGDON VIRGINIA
APRIL 20th 1809
DIED IN
COLUMBIA, SOUTH CAROLINA
MAY 1st 1881
(RC-52)

SACRED TO THE MEMORY
OF FREDERICK SCHAFFNER
LOST AT SEA ON HIS PASSAGE
FROM NEW ORLEANS TO CHARLESTON
IN THE SCHOONER *PEE DEE*,
CAPTAIN GEORGE TOLSON
IN A HEAVY GALE, ON THE 15TH
OF AUGUST, OFF THE TORTUGAS.
BORN IN SCHWEINFURT GERMANY
AGED FORTY NINE YEARS.
(CT-76)

IN MEMORY OF
JOHN WHITE
BORN IN COUNTY ANTRIM
IRELAND 1720
WITH HIS WIFE ANN WHITE
AND THEIR CHILDREN CAME
TO CHESTER COUNTY IN 1767
THE DATE OF HIS DEATH
PRIOR TO THE REVOLUTIONARY
WAR IS UNKNOWN
(CS-9)

JOHN RUSK
BUILDER OF
OLD STONE CHURCH
MARY STERRITT
WIFE OF
JOHN RUSK
1797
MOTHER AND FATHER OF
THOMAS JEFFERSON RUSK
1803 – 1857

PIONEER, SOLDIER, STATESMAN
OF TEXAS
ERECTED BY THE STATE OF TEXAS
1836
(PK-8)

SACRED TO THE MEMORY
OF FREDERICK ANONE
THE ELDEST SON OF F. ANONE
WHO DEPARTED THIS LIFE
ON THE 19th OCTOBER
1817
AGED 15 YEARS &
3 MONTHS
A NATIVE OF LONDON

IN PRIDE OF YOUTH IN LIFE'S MOST FLATTERING
BLOOM,
WITH EVERY GENEROUS SENTIMENT INSPIRED,
HE SUNK REGRETTED TO AN EARLY TOMB,
AND FROM HIS TENDER PARENTS DEAR EXPIRED.
(BF-10)

HERE REST THE BODY
OF
MR. WILLIAM BLAIR
WHO DEPARTED THIS LIFE IN THE 66TH YEAR OF HIS
AGE
ON THE 2ND OF JULY A.D. 1821 AT 9 O'CLOCK PM
HE WAS BORN IN THE COUNTY OF ANTRIM IRELAND
ON THE 24TH OF MARCH 1759. WHEN ABOUT 13 YEARS
OLD
HE CAME WITH HIS FATHER & FAMILY TO THIS
COUNTRY
WHERE HE RESIDED TILL HIS DEATH.
IMMEDIATELY ON THE LEFT ARE DEPOSITED THE
EARTHLY
REMAINS OF HIS ONLY WIFE SARAH, WHOSE DEATH
PRECEDED HIS OWN BUT A FEW YEARS.
HE WAS A REVOLUTIONARY PATRIOT. AND IN
THE HUMBLE STATIONS OF PRIVATE SOLDIER AND
WAGON MASTER IT IS BELIEVED HE CONTRIBUTED
MORE ESSENTIALLY TO THE ESTABLISHMENT
OF AMERICAN
INDEPENDENCE THAN MANY WHOSE NAMES ARE
PROUDLY EMBLAZONED ON THE PAGES OF HISTORY.
WITH HIS FATHER'S WAGON HE ASSISTED IN
TRANSPORTING THE BAGGAGE OF THE AMERICAN
ARMY FOR SEVERAL MONTHS. HE WAS ALSO
IN THE BATTLES OF THE HANGING ROCK, THE EUTAW,
RATLIFF'S BRIDGE, STONO AND THE
FISH DAM FORD OM THE BROAD RIVER. IN ONE
OF THESE BATTLES (IT IS NOT RECOLLECTED WHICH)
HE
RECEIVED A SLIGHT WOUND; BUT SO FAR FROM
REGARDING IT, EITHER THEN OR AFTERWARDS, WHEN
IT WAS INTIMATED TO HIM THAT HE MIGHT AVAIL
HIMSELF OF THE BOUNTY OF HIS COUNTRY, AND
DRAW A PENSION (AS MANY OF HIS CAMP ASSOCIATES
HAD DONE) HE DECLARED THAT, IF THE SMALL

COMPETENCE HE THEN POSSESSED FAILED HIM, HE
WAS BOTH ABLE AND WILLING TO WORK FOR HIS
LIVING; AND IF IT BECAME NECESSARY, TO FIGHT
FOR HIS COUNTRY WITHOUT A PENNY OF PAY.
HE IN THE LANGUAGE OF POPE.
THE NOBLEST WORK OF GOD, AN HONEST MAN.
"NO FATHER SEEKS HIS MERITS TO DISCLOSE
OR DRAW HIS FRAILTIES FROM THEIR DREAD ABODE
(THERE THEY ALIKE IN TREMBLING HOPE REPOSE)
THE BOSOM OF HIS FATHER AND HIS GOD"
(LC-7)

GEORGE WILLIAM WITTE
A NATIVE OF
HANNOVER GERMANY
DECEMBER 14TH 1831
SEPTEMBER 2ND 1893
*"ICH HABE DICH ERLÖSET;
ICH HABE DICH BEI
DEINEM NAMEN GERUFEN, DU BIST MEIN"
(CT-93)

*I have thee as my Saviour
I have called thee
By thy name, thou art mine*

DR. CHARLES C. A. ZIMMERMAN
A NATIVE OF GERMANY
AND FOR MANY YEARS A CITIZEN
OF THE UNITED STATES
DIED DEC. 3, 1867
HIS LIFE WAS DEVOTED TO
LITERATURE AND USEFUL
PURPOSES
(RC-33)

IN MEMORY OF
MRS. MARIA WISE
WIFE OF
ALFRED WISE
A NATIVE OF ISLINGTON MIDDLESEX;
LONDON, ENGLAND
SHE DEPARTED THIS LIFE APRIL 22ND 1861
IN THE 61rst YEAR OF HER AGE

SHE WAS __ BUT WORDS ARE WANTING,
TO SAY WHAT__ SAY WHAT A WIFE
SHOULD BE __ AND SHE WAS THAT.
(CT-94)

SACRED TO THE MEMORY
OF
GEORGE WAGNER JUNR.
ELDEST SON OF
GEORGE AND CHARLOTTE O. WAGNER.
WHO WAS BORN 19TH SEPTR. 1817
AND DIED ON BOARD SHIP ALBATROSS
DURING HIS VOYAGE
FROM CALCUTTA TO LIVERPOOL
ON HIS RETURN HOME.
THE 11TH APRIL 1843

LET US LISTEN TO A VOICE
AS IT WERE FROM HEAVEN;
IF YE LOVE ME YE WILL REJOICE,
FOR I GO TO MY FATHER.
(CT-31)

IN MEMORY OF
WILLIAM A. BROWN
BORN IN COLA., S. C. JULY 23rd 1832.
MOVED WITH HIS PARENTS TO ALA. 1841
VOLUNTEERED IN THE CONFEDERATE
SERVICE MAY 1862, WAS A MEMBER OF
CP. D. 42nd REGT. ALA. VOLS.
FOUGHT IN MANY BATTLES
OF THE WEST, WAS WOUNDED AND
CAPTURED IN THE BATTLE OF
MISSIONARY RIDGE, WAS HELD A PRISONER
10 MO. ON ACCOUNT OF ILL HEALTH
WAS PAROLED, REACHED HIS NATIVE
CITY AND WITHIN SIX DAYS AFTER HIS
ARRIVAL IN THE HOUSE IN WHICH HE
WAS BORN, DIED OCTOBER 9th 1864.
HE WAS A DUTIFUL SON, KIND AND
AFFECTIONATE BROTHER, AND ENJOYED
THE ESTEEM OF ALL WHO KNEW HIM.
HE SLEEPS HIS LAST SLEEP, HE HAS FOUGHT
HIS LAST FIGHT.
(RC-10)

SAUL SOLOMONS
WHO DIED ON THE
1ST MARCH 1843
IN ABOUT THE 72ND YEAR OF HIS AGE
HE WAS BORN IN LEIPSIC [LEIPZIG], GERMANY,
BUT FOR UPWARDS OF THE LAST 50 YEARS HE
RESIDED IN COLLETON AND BEAUFORT
DISTRICTS ABOUT 45 OF WHICH IN THE LATTER.
(HM-11)

CHAPTER 2

SO YOUNG & SO DEAR

That's All Folks! The Man of a Thousand Voices

Epitaph of Mel Blanc

SACRED
TO THE MEMORY OF
JANE REBECCA
FIRST DAUGHTER
AND SECOND CHILD OF
DR. JAMES B. & MARY E. DAVIS
SHE WAS BORN FEBRUARY 6th
1834
AND DEPARTED THIS LIFE
JUNE 14th 1839

REST CALMLY CHERUB CHILD WITHIN
THY LITTLE LONELY GRAVE,
THY DOUBTING FRIENDS NOW WEEP FOR
THEY STROVE IN VAIN TO SAVE.
(FF-2)

MARION
INFANT DAUGHTER
OF
J. S. & H. I. COLES
DIED MAR. 15, 1885
BUT FOR A MOMENT
FELT THE ROD.
(RC-48)

OUR BABE
EDITH C. FORDE
BORN
OCT. 29, 1876,
DIED
AUG. 6, 1877.
EDITH IS AN ANGEL NOW.
(RC-43)

SACRED
TO THE MEMORY
OF
MARY FISHER
TWIN DAUGHTER OF
MALCOM A. & MARY F. SHELTON
WHO WAS BORN
NOVEMBER 30th 1851,
AND DEPARTED THIS LIFE
DECEMBER 20th 1852.
AGED 1 YEAR 20 DAYS
UNDERNEATH THE SOD LOW LYING
DARK AND DREAR,
SLEEPETH ONE WHO LEFT IN DYING
SORROW HERE.
(RC-47)

SACRED
TO THE MEMORY OF
JAMES BELL
WHO DEPARTED THIS LIFE
ON THE 18th OF NOV. 1809
IN THE SEVENTH YEAR OF HIS AGE
SLEEP ON DEAR BOY, TILL ANGELS
SHARE THY TOMB;
AND KINDRED SPIRITS CALL
THEE TO THY HOME.
THAN WILL THOU BURST THE
BANDS OF DEATH AND RISE
TO MEET THY SAVIOUR IN THE
ETHEREAL SKIES.
(FF-10)

SACRED
TO THE MEMORY OF
SARAH ANTOINETT
INFANT DAUGHTER
OF J.T. & S.A. STEELE
DIED AUGUST THE
10th 1858 - AGED 7
MONTHS & 5 DAYS

SWEET BABE
*THY MOTHER LEFT THEE
AT THY BIRTH
AN ORPHAN TO SMILE,
OR TO WEEP,
SHE SMILED NOT
ON HER INFANT CHILD
HER SPIRIT TOOK ITS FATE.
(PK-1)

*Her mother died in childbirth and she was buried next to her.

OUR LITTLE DON
DIED JAN 28, 1892
AGED 3 YRS. 2 MOS. & 5 DAYS

LEAVES HAVE THEIR TIME TO FALL
AND FLOWERS TO WITHER AT THE
NORTH WINDS BREATH.
AND STARS TO SET - BUT ALL.
THOU HAST ALL SEASONS FOR
THINE OWN, OH DEATH.
(BF-9)

IN MEMORY OF
SAMUEL MICHAEL
FIRST SON OF DANIEL
THOMAS & RUDELLA
ELIZABETH BARR,
WHO WAS BORN DEC. 10th 1851,
AND DIED SEPT. 13th 1856,
AGED 4 YEARS 9 MONTHS
AND 3 DAYS.

MY LITTLE ONE, MY FAIR ONE,
THOU CANST NOT COME TO ME,
BUT NEARER DRAWS THE NUMBERED
HOUR WHEN I SHALL GO TO THEE.
AND THOUGH PERCHANCE WITH SERAPH
SMILE AND GOLDEN HARP IN HAND,
MAYEST COME THE FIRST TO WELCOME
ME TO OUR EMANUEL'S LAND.
(LX-2)

WILLIAM PATRICK HENDRIX
BORN
FEBRUARY 9th, 1857,
DIED
SEPT. 17th, 1863.
MAKING HIS WHOLE LIFE
6 YEARS, 7 MONTHS & 8 DAYS.

SWEET BE THY REST 'O' WILLIE,
TO MEET AGAIN WE CRAVE;
ALL WE CAN DO IS MORN THY LOSS,
UNTIL WE MEET IN HEAVEN.
(RC-18)

LILA MAE VIRGINIA
DAUGHTER OF
MR. & MRS. T. H. ALLEN
BORN FEB. 13, 1915
DIED OCT. 22, 1918
THIS FAIR SWEET FLOWER IN
PARADISE SHALL BLOOM
(RC-2)

RUTH B.
DAUGHTER OF
T. H. & E. R. ALLEN
JUNE 7, 1913
MAY 22, 1915

THE LITTLE FEET IN THE GOLDEN STREET
SHALL NEVER GO ASTRAY
(RC-3)

ROBERT
SON OF
THOS. & ELIZABETH H. BOYNE.
BORN JANY. 26th 1851.
ACCIDENTALLY DROWNED
AUGUST 18th 1857.
HE WAS SO DEAR TO US - SO GOOD,
SO BEAUTIFUL AND FAIR;
WITH HIS KIND EYES AND PLEASANT SMILES
AND HIS SOFT WAVING HAIR;
AND HE TO DIE, NOR WE BE THERE
TO LISTEN TO HIS FERVENT PRAYER.
(RC-22)

CONSTANCE DeSAUSSURE
AGE 17 MONTHS 25 DAYS
NO SIN COULD BLIGHT OR SORROW FADE.
DEATH CAME WITH FRIENDLY CARE.
THE OPENING BUDS TO HEAVEN CONVEYED
AND BADE THEM BLOSSOM THERE.
(RC-29)

DIED MARCH 3RD 1868
CHARLES GIGNILLIAT
SON OF
DR. E. & LAURA GEDDINGS
AGED 5 YEARS 11 DAYS

"WITH THY GOING WENT THE SUN
FROM MY SKY,
LEAVING UPON MY PATH A NIGHT
ETERNALLY!!"
……..HIS MOTHER
(CT-87)

HERE LYETH THE BODY OF
JOHN GERLEY SON OF
MR. JOHN GERLEY
WHO DEPARTED THIS LIFE
THE 17TH DAY OF MAY A.D. 1769
AGE 22 MONTHS
(OUR LOVE IS EVER ON THE WING,
AND DEATH IS EVER NIGH
THE MOMENT WHEN OUR LIVES BEGIN
WE ALL BEGIN TO DIE)
(CT-56)

SACRED
TO THE MEMORY OF
BENJAMIN FRANKLIN McKEE
WHO DIED THE 21ST APRIL 1835
AGED NINE YEARS FIVE MONTHS
AND SEVEN DAYS

SACRED
TO THE MEMORY OF
JULIA FALICIA McKEE
WHO DIED THE 20TH APRIL 1835
AGED SEVEN YEARS THREE MONTHS
AND FOURTEEN DAYS

SACRED
TO THE MEMORY OF
HAYDEN McKEE
WHO DIED 26TH APRIL 1835
AGED TWO YEARS, NINE MONTHS

SACRED
TO THE MEMORY OF
AN INFANT DAUGHTER
WHO DIED 22ND MARCH 1835
AGED THREE DAYS

SACRED
TO THE MEMORY OF
WILLIAM DRAYTON McKEE
WHO DIED THE 20TH OF APRIL 1835
AGED FIVE YEARS THREE MONTHS
AND EIGHTEEN DAYS

FOUR DIED IN ONE WEEK
TWO OF THEM IN ONE DAY
AND ONE BUT FOUR WEEKS BEFORE'

THE ABOVE CHILDREN OF
JOHN & MARY McKEE
WERE ALL BORN AND DIED AT CHESTERFIELD, So.Ca.
FEW PARENTS
HAVE SUFFERED THUS
HARD FATE WHY WAS IT SO?
(CS-2)

MANNING M. LANDRUM
DIED FEB. 3rd 1831
AT AGE 1 YEAR 2 MONTHS 16 DAYS

"DEAR LITTLE SAFFERER FARE THEE WELL,
BORNE FROM A PARENT'S ARMS WITH THY GODDE.
DWELL IN HAPPIER REALMS, NO MORE TO FEAR,
THE SORE AFFLICTIONS SUFFERED HERE."
(RC-30)

VIRGINIA CELESTE TALLEY,
AGED 8 YEARS, 6 MONTHS
AND 24 DAYS
OBIT
FEB. 17th 1875
YOUNGEST
BELOVED CHILD OF
A. N. & E. P. TALLEY

YES, THOU ART GONE, ERE GRIEF HAD POWER
TO STAIN THY CHERUB FACE OR FORM;
CLOSED IS THE SOFTEST EPHEM'RAL FLOWER
THAT NEVER FELT THE STORM
(RC-55)

IN MEMORY
OF
OUR YOUNG FRIEND
HARRIET BEE
BORN AUGUST 9TH 1844
DIED JANUARY 6TH 1853
AGED 9 YEARS, 4 MONTHS, 26 DAYS.

AND WHILST THOU PART OUR LITTLE FRIEND;
TO SEEK GOD WHO WILL ATTEND;
ALAS, TIS TRUE YOU MUST DECEASE
OH' PART LITTLE FRIEND ADIEU IN PEACE.
(CT-16)

BENEATH THIS STONE
LIE THE REMAINS OF
EMMA CARROLL,
WHO DIED JAN. 23d 1839
AGED 4 YEARS, 26 DAYS
AND OF HER
INFANT SISTER,
WHO DIED NOV. 10TH 1835
DAUGHTERS OF B.R. AND ELIZA A. CARROLL

THE FLOWERS RIPEN'D BLOOM UMATCH'D
MUST FALL THE EARLIEST PREY;
THOUGH BY NO HAND UNTIMELY SNATCH'D
THE LEAVES MUST DROP AWAY;
AND YET IT WORE A GREATER GRIEF
TO WATCH IT WITHERING LEAF BY LEAF
THAN SEE IT PLUCK'D TODAY.
(CT-17)

HERE LIES THE BODIES OF THREE BROTHERS
SONS OF RICHARD AND MARY SAVAGE
WHO WERE INTERRED WITHIN TEN DAYS
CLOSE TO THIS STONE

JOHN CLIFFORD SAVAGE DIED
AUGUST 31rst 1784 AGED 7 YEARS, 5 MO. & 7 DAYS

WILLIAM SAVAGE SEPTEMBER 8th
1784 AGED 3 YEARS, 6 MO.

DANDRIDGE RICHARD SAVAGE
SEPTEMBER 9th 1784, AGED 5 YEARS, 6 MO. & 6 DAYS

BENEATHE THE SURFACE OF THIS TURFED EARTH
ENWRAPT IN SILENCE AND THE ARMS OF DEATH
EXPOSED TO WORMS LIES 3 ONCE CHARMING BOYS
THE FATHER'S COMFORT AND THE MOTHER'S JOY
THESE YOUTHS AT ONCE FAIR FRUIT
AND BLOSSOMS BORE
MUCH IN POSSESSION IN EXPECTANCE MORE
THOU'D GRIEVE YOU TENDER READER TO RELATE
THE HASTY STRIDES OF UNRELENTING FATE
THE POWER OF MEDICINE FALL'D THE HEALING TRAIT
BUT HAPPY YOUTHS BY DEATH MADE TRULY GREAT
HAD LIFE BEEN LENGTHEN'D TO IT'S UTMOST DATE
WHAT HAD THEY KNOWN BUT SORROW, PAIN & WOE
THE CURSE ENTAILED ON ADAMS RACE BELOW
THEYRE ONLY SAFE WHO THRO
DEATH'S GATES HAVE PASS'D
& REACHED THOSE JOYS THAT EVER MORE WILL HAST
HOW FAIN IS MAN, HOW FLUTTERING ARE HIS JOYS
WHEN WHAT ONE MOMENT GIVES
THE NEXT DESTROYS
HOPE AND DESPAIR FILL UP HIS ROUND OF LIFE
AND ALL OF HIS JOYS ARE ONE CONTINUAL STRIFE
(CT-54)

SAMUEL GUILDS SEABROOK, III
DEC 17, 1966 – JAN 27, 1969
A CHERUB WAS NEEDED IN HEAVEN TODAY
SO REST THE INNOCENCE WHERE THIS CHILD LAY.
(CT-6)

C.H.W.
AGED 21 MONTHS
DIED
APRIL 10TH 1855
CAROLINE
"EARLY, BRIGHT, TRANSIENT,
CHASTE AS MORNING DEW,
SHE SPARKLED, WAS EXALTED,
AND WENT TO HEAVEN."
(CT-61)

CHARLOTTE LOUISA CUDWORTH
BORN
MARCH 25, 1902
DIED SEPT 12, 1903
"ROCK-A-BYE, BABY"
(CT-57)

SACRED
TO THE MEMORY OF
CAROLINI M. DESEL
WHO DIED SEPTEMBER THE 22
1799 AGED 1 YEAR AND 9 MONTHS
"SLEEP LOVELY BABE AND TAKE THY REST
GOD CALLED THEE EARLY BECAUSE HE LIKED THEE
BEST"
(CT-74)

SACRED TO THE MEMORY OF
JULIA ELIZABETH
SECOND CHILD OF BENJ. H. & EMMA A.
BARFIELD
BORN 15TH MARCH 1849
DIED 3RD MARCH 1856
AGED 6 YEARS 11 MONTHS AND 18 DAYS
THIS DEAR AND INTERESTING CHILD
WAS MEEKLY AND INNOCENTLY ASCENDING
THE HILL OF LIFE BUT WHEN SHE HAD
NEARLY REACHED HER SEVENTH YEAR
SWEET JESUS CALLED AND SHE HASTENED HOME
B.H. MARCH 3, 1856
JULIA E. BARFIELD
7 YEARS, NATIVE OF CHARLESTON
(CT-49)

MARY JANE TO LITTLE
ADA MOORE
AGED 8 MONTHS
13 DAYS
SHE CAME
AND FADED LIKE A
WREATH OF MIST AT EVE'
(AB-9)

BOULWARE
LOVINGLY CALLED "MINNIE"
APRIL 24, 1856
SEPT, 21, 1954
(CS-3)

IN
MEMORY
OF
A STILL BORN INFANT
SON OF WM. D &
C.E. HENRY
BORN
ON THE 26TH DAY
1831
"SLEEP ON MY BABE."
(CS-8)

OUR LITTLE
EDDIE
ONLY SON OF D. H.
AND ELIZA KELLY
DIED AUG. 9, 1873.
AGED 3 YEARS.
ONE SWEET FLOWER HAS DROOPT AND FADED
ONE SWEET INFANT VOICE HAS FLED
ONE FAIR BROW THE GRAVE HAS SHADED
ONE DEAR OBJECT NOW IS DEAD.
(RC-45)

EMMA
DAUGHTER OF
J.T. & M.D. HOWERTON
WAS BORN FEB 3RD 1840
DIED
JULY 9TH 1845
AGED 5 YEARS
5 MONTHS AND 6 DAYS
"HALF UNOPENED BUD OF INNOCENCE
(CS-7)

OUR LITTLE LILLY
BELOVED CHILD OF
MOTTE AND MARY ALSTON
WHO
"FELL ASLEEP IN JESUS"
ON THE MORNING OF 4th DEC.
1861
AGED 2 YEARS
AND 21 DAYS
"FOLD HER, OH FATHER, IN THINE ARMS,
AND LET HER HENCEFORTH BE
A MESSENGER OF LOVE, BETWEEN
OUR HUMAN HEARTS AND THEE."
(RC-60)

IN
MEMORY OF
AN INFANT DAUGHTER OF
JOHN AND JANE E, MOORE
WHO DIED AUGUST 18TH 1841
AGED 21 HOURS
SLEEP LITTLE BABY SLEEP,
NOT IN THY CRADLE BED
NOT ON THY MOTHERS BREAST
BUT IN THE QUIET DEAD
HE TOOK THEE IN HIS MERCY
YOUNG, UNLASHED, UNTRIED
FOR ALL WITH HIM IS PARADISE
AND THE SANCTIFIED
(CS-6)

SACRED
TO THE MEMORY OF
ESTELLE,
THE DAUGHTER OF
CONSTANTINE AND ELIZABETH
BAILEY
WHO DEPARTED THIS LIFE
ON THE 13TH OF AUGUST
1852
AGED 1 YEAR, 7 MONTHS
AND 18 DAYS

AS SOMETHING SHADOWY AND FRAIL,
WAS NEVER IN HER MIRTH;
SHE LOOKED A FLOWER, THAT ONE ROUGH GALE,
MIGHT BEAR AWAY FROM EARTH.
(CT-7)

JOSEPH E. HEAPE
1890 - 1890
PARADISE WANTED MOTHERS SPRING FLOWER
(HM-3)

41

CHAPTER 3

PROSE FROM THE PANTHEON

Coffin-board, heavy stone,
Lie on her breast,
I vex my heart alone
She is at rest.

Peace, Peace, she cannot hear
Lyre or sonnet,
All my life's buried here,
Heap earth upon it.

From "Requiescat" by Oscar Wilde

MARGAN KANE
DIED
APRIL 30, 1901
AGED 81 YEARS

AN ORPHAN YET AN HEIR
OF GOD.
(AL-4)

JOHN LAIRD
BORN GLASCOW SCOTLAND
OCT. 16, 1846
DIED AIKEN, S. C. FEB. 27, 1928.
MATTIE H. PERCIVAL LAIRD
BORN COLUMBIA, S. C. JULY 18, 1851
DIED AIKEN, S. C. JAN. 20, 1928

WARM SUMMER SUN SHINE KINDLY HERE
WARM SOUTHERN WIND BLOW SOFTLY HERE
GREEN SOD ABOVE LIE LIGHT, LIE LIGHT,
GOOD NIGHT DEAR HEARTS, GOOD NIGHT.
GOOD NIGHT!
(AK-2)

SARAH ELIZABETH
KIRKLAND

"TWENTY BEAUTIFUL
YEARS"
MARCH 19, 1878 - JULY 1, 1898
(BB-1)

CAPT. JOS. DUNCAN
MRS. H. W. DUNCAN
ONCE HAPPY COUPLE

WHILE MEMORY FAITHFUL MOVES THE MOURNFUL
SOUL,
AND LIFE'S WARM CURRENTS TRUE TO NATURE ROLL.
LAMENTED SPIRITS ON THY CLAY COLD BED,
THY SONS AND ONLY DAUGHTER'S TRIBUTE SHALL BE
SHED.
(BW-1)

GLADYS
SHE WAS FROM GOD___HE
HAS CLAIMED HIS OWN.
HER LIFE OF THE PUREST WAY,
BLUSHED INTO THE DAY.
TOOMER
(BF-4)

IN MEMORY
OF
JAMES HIRAM
STURDEVANT
1884 - 1948

----

*"MY LABOR'S DONE"
(BF-5)

* This headstone had a copper sundial mounted to it with
the inscription: *When Sinks Ye Sun, My Labor's Done*

44

HANNAH HEYWARD
TRAPIER
WIFE OF
ARTHUR POSTELL
JERVY
JUNE 18, 1857
MAY 13, 1935
"THE LOVELIEST AND THE BEST"
(CT-91)

WILLIAM ELLIOTT
BORN BEAUFORT, S. C.
MARCH 30, 1872
DIED COLUMBIA, S. C.
APRIL 6, 1943

HOME IS THE SAILOR
HOME FROM THE SEA
AND THE HUNTER HOME
FROM THE HILL
(BF-6)

IN MEMORY
OF
MARTHA E. WILSON
CONSORT OF
ROBERT WILSON
WHO DIED 1st OCT. 1850
AGED 45 YEARS
AFFLICTED BY MY LOSS, I LAY THEE HERE,
IN SILENT SORROW: THY DUST IS DEAR,
FOR NEVER CHILD SHALL WEEP, NOR NEIGHBOUR
BEND,
O'VER KINDER PARENT OR MORE FAITHFUL FRIEND.
(KS-11)

ADAM TEAM
BORN
JAN 5, 1831
DIED OCT 8, 1891
I THINK I HEAR THY
GENTLE VOICE,
FROM CANAAN'S
HAPPY SHORE;
IT WHISPERS, TRUST IN
GOD MY WIFE,
AND WEEP FOR ME NO MORE.
(KS-10)

ELIZA SEABROOK
HAY
APR. 14, 1860
AUG. 27, 1929
"AN EVENTIDE – AT REST."
(CT-15)

SACRED
TO THE MEMORY OF
MRS. SALLIE H. NETTLES
WIFE OF
WILLIAM A. NETTLES,
AGED 26 YEARS
"LO WHERE THE SILENT MARBLE WEEPS,
A FRIEND, A WIFE, A MOTHER SLEEPS.
A HEART WITHIN WHOSE SACRED CELL,
THE PEACEFUL VIRTUES LOVE'D TO DWELL.
AFFECTION WARM AND FAITH SINCERE,
AND SOFT HUMANITY WERE THERE"
(KS-12)

SACRED TO THE MEMORY
OF
ALFRED BREVARD,
WHO DEPARTED THIS LIFE ON THE
FOURTEENTH OF SEPTEMBER 1836
IN THE FORTY SECOND YEAR
OF HIS AGE
WHEN SORROWING O'ER HIS TOMB I BEND,
WHICH COVERS ALL THAT WAS A FRIEND,
AND FROM HIS VOICE, HIS HAND, HIS SMILE,
DIVIDES ME FOR A LITTLE WHILE;
THOU SAVIOR SEE'ST THE TEARS I SHED,
FOR THOU DID'ST WEEP O'ER A FRIEND DEAD,
THEN POINT TO REALMS OF ENDLESS DAY,
AND WIPE THE LATEST TEAR AWAY.
(KS-13)

GEORGE JACKSON
SON OF
GEORGE & RACHEL S. JACKSON,
BORN JUNE 7TH 1828,
DIED AUGUST 10TH 1860
EVERY WIND THAT BLOWETH,
WHISPERS THY NAME
(CT-92)

CHARLOTTE T. YARBOROUGH.
1853 – 1892
TIS' ONLY THE CASKET THAT LIES HERE
THE GEM THAT FILLED IT OPERATES YET.
(FF-1)

SACRED TO THE MEMORY
OF
JOSHUA PLAYER
WHO DEPARTED THIS LIFE
ON THE 21st
OF NOVEMBER 1833
AGED FIFTY FIVE YEARS

WE'VE NO ABIDING CITY HERE
WE SEEK A CITY OUT OF SIGHT
ZION IT'S NAME, THE LORD IS THERE
IT SHINES WITH EVERLASTING LIGHT.
(FF-8)

SACRED
TO THE MEMORY OF
CHARLES MONTGOMERY
WHO DEPARTED THIS LIFE
ON THE 27 DAY OF OCTOBER 1820
IN THE 72d YEAR OF HIS AGE

SWIFT DO OUR DAYS AND YEARS ROLL ON
TO FINISH NATURES PLAN,
TILL DEATH'S BOLD CALL DOTH CLOSE THE SCENE
AND MISERY OF MAN
LET NOT THIS FLEETING MOMENT PASS
FOR TIME MAKES NO DELAY
YOU KNOW NOT WHEN THIS CALL MAY COME
PREPARE THEN WHILST YOU MAY.
(FF-9)

INSCRIBED
TO THE MEMORY OF
JOHN WENTWORTH BLACK
WHO DIED 16TH AUGUST 1827
AGED 19 YEARS AND 3 DAYS
THO SEEN NO MORE ON EARTH,
THOU WAST DEAR,
TO FRIENDS WHO KNEW THEE,
WEPT THY EARLY DOOM,
OFT SHALL THY FORM,
TO FANCY'S EYE APPEAR,
AND MEM'RY LOVE,
TO LINGER ROUND THY TOMB.
(CT-27)

BLAKE L.
WHITE,
SEPT. 20, 1842
MAY 5, 1905
TON ÉPOUSE ET AMIE
ROSALIE
(CT-103)

Your Wife and Friend Rosalie

CAROL SETZLER HARLEY, Ph.D.
NOV. 8, 1940 - JAN. 31, 1986

FOR THY SWEET LOVE REMEMBERED SUCH
WEALTH BRINGS, THAT THEN I SCORN TO
CHANGE MY STATE WITH KINGS.
(NB-5)

Front side:

CARRIE C. DUNCAN
WIFE OF
D. P. DUNCAN
DAUGHTER OF
EX. GOV. & M.E. GIST
DIED AUG'T 19TH 1876
AGED 32 YEARS, 10 MO's
& 19 D'YS

Right side:

"SHE IS AN ANGEL NOW, TO
HER APPEAR,
THE WISHED FOR JOYS OF
HEAVEN'S ETERNAL YEAR."

Left side:

"HER MEMORY IS THE SHRINE
OF PLEASANT THOUGHT,
SOFT AS THE SCENT OF
FLOWERS,
RICH AS THE RAINBOW WITH
IT'S ARCH OF LIGHT
PURE AS THE MOONSHINE OF
AN AUTUMN NIGHT"

Back side:

"BELOVED, WE SHALL
MEET AGAIN"
(UN-2)

ELLEN
BELOVED WIFE OF
J. STUART LAND
DIED NOV. 18, 1878
AGED 24 YEARS

ELLEN WILL BLOOM AGAIN.
(RC-32)

Front side:

KEELS
ELIZABETH RICHARDSON
OCT. 16 1919
NOV.16 1987
&
RALF ERNEST
NOV. 26 1909

Back side:

MY WOODLAND CATHEDRAL
I LIFT UP MINE EYES AND PEACE AS DEEP AS PLACID
WATER FLOWS INTO MY SOUL.
THE GOD I SEEK IS NEAR AT HAND.
I SEE HIM IN THE TALL, STRAIGHT TREES, THE BENT
GNARLED THAT HAVE KNOWN HIS HANDIWORK
THROUGH TIME AND AGE AND STORM.
I HEAR HIM AS HE MOVES ACROSS THE BURNT BROWN
NEEDLES OF PINE.
OH LORD, THOU HAST KNOWN ME AND SEEN ME.
I AM NAKED BEFORE THEE,
MY ARMS REACH UP, BUT MY HEAD IS BOWED IN
WONDER AT THE POWER AND THY GLORY ON THE EARTH.
I COME TO THEE IN MY WOODLAND CATHEDRAL AND I
AM CLEANSED.   AMEN.
Who's who among American poets 1984 - E. R. K.
(SM-1)

IN MEMORY OF
ALEXANDER CAIRNS
WHO DIED OCT. 19, 1801
AGED 23 YEARS

BUT I AM IN THE HOUSE OF GOD
LIKE TO AN OLIVE GREEN,
MY CONFIDENCE FOREVER HATH
UPON GOD'S MERCIES BEEN
(LC-6)

PHILLIP P. COUTORIER
KIRK
DECEMBER 31, 1860
OCTOBER 24, 1925
THE DEAD ARE AS
THE STARS BY DAY
(SM-2)

MARY MARINA
LONG,
WIFE OF
JACOB B. LONG
DEC. 10, 1850
AUG. 24, 1926
THE ROSE MAY FADE, THE LILLIE DIE
BUT THIS FLOWER IS IMMORTAL.
(NB-1)

SACRED
TO THE MEMORY OF
M. M. ELIZABETH FOLK.
WIFE OF
LEVI E. FOLK
WHO WAS BORN
OCTOBER 15th 1831,
AND DIED
NOVEMBER 9th 1860

LIKE ONE WHO DRAWS THE DRAPERY OF HER COUCH
ABOUT HER, AND LIES DOWN TO PLEASANT DREAMS.
(NB-2)

SAMUEL CARY BECKWITH
NOV. 17, 1870 – JAN. 2, 1939
RECTOR AND RECTOR EMERITUS
ST. PHILIP'S CHURCH, 1906 – 1939
"LIKE SOME GREAT RIVER WINDING TO THE SEA;
BROADLY AND GRANDLY, SILENTLY AND DEEP;
LIFE JOINS ETERNITY"
(CT-35)

IRVINE KEITH HEYWARD
BORN JUNE 26, 1840
OBT. SEP. 21, 1880
THERE IS NO DEATH!
WHAT SEEMS SO IS TRANSITION
THIS LIFE OF MORTAL BREATH
IS BUT A SUBURB
OF THE LIFE ELYSIAN
WHOSE PORTAL WE CALL DEATH
(CT-84)

HERE LIETH INTERRD
THE BODY OF
MRS. SARAH CREIGHTON
WIFE OF WILLIAM CREIGHTON
RELICT OF JOHN BUTLER PIGGATT
AND DAUGHTER OF
JOHN & MARTHA CLIFFORD
WHO DEPARTED THIS LIFE
THE 1rst OF JANY 1775 AGED
36 YEARS & 5 MONTHS

"THIS MORTAL LIFE DECAYS APACE,
HOW SOON THE BUBBLES BROKE,
ADAM AND ALL HIS NUMEROUS RACE,
ARE VANITY AND SMOAK"
(CT-36)

FATHER
JAMES THOMAS FETNER
JANUARY 15, 1847
MARCH 10, 1908
MOTHER
ELIZABETH ANNE MILNE
WIFE OF
JAMES THOMAS FETNER
MARCH 1, 1852
AUGUST 7, 1934
HOW SWEET IT WILL BE IN THAT BEAUTIFUL LAND,
FREE FROM ALL SORROW AND PAIN,
WITH SONGS ON OUR LIPS,
AND WITH HARPS IN OUR HANDS,
WE SHALL MEET ONE ANOTHER AGAIN.
(RC-12)

TO THE MEMORY OF
WILMOT DeSAUSSURE
PORCHER
SEPT 14, 1860
JULY 25, 1925
I GIVE THEE BACK THE LIFE I OWE
THAT IN THINE OCEAN DEPTHS ITS FLOW
MAY RICHER FULLER BE
(CT-85)

MAJ. JOHN KENNEDY
BORN FEBY 12TH 1770
DIED APRIL 7TH 1867
AGED 97 YEARS 1 MO. 26 DAYS
"THOU SHALT BE MISSED
BECAUSE THY SEAT WILL BE EMPTY"
(CS-14)

HERE LIES MY WIFE
THE BLOOM OF MY LIFE,
AND MY CHILD IN THE
GRAVE WITH ITS MOTHER.
WIFE OF W. W. HAYGOOD,
DAUGHTER EMILY
OF JOHN DARRAGH,
BORN
JULY 10, 1861;
MARRIED
JUNE 11, 1885;
DIED
DEC. 17, 1890.
(AB-7)

OSCAR E. HUGHES.
MARCH 13, 1856 - AUGUST 15, 1908

REST MY DARLING, LIFE'S FEVER ENDED.
SLEEP IN PEACE BENEATH THE SOD
AS THY GLAD SOUL FLIES, ATTENDED
BY BRIGHT ANGELS UP TO GOD.
"BY HIS WIFE MATTIE"
(RC-13)

T. W. BERRY
MAR. 15, 1860
NOV. 21, 1911

THE PAINS OF DEATH ARE PAST,
LABOR AND SORROW CEASED,
AND LIFE'S WARFARE CLOSED AT LAST
HIS SOUL IS FOUND IN PEACE.
(RC-14)

JANE A.
WIFE OF D. B. SLOAN,
BORN
MARCH 28, 1864
DIED
MAY 12, 1899

THERE IS NO DEATH! THE STARS
GO DOWN TO RISE UPON SOME
FAIRER SHORE.
(RC-15)

IN
MEMORY OF
THEODORE VOGEL
WHO WAS BORN
MAY 8, 1820
AND DIED
SEPT. 1ST, 1862

HE WAS A USEFUL CITIZEN, A KIND NEIGHBOUR
AND AFFECTIONATE HUSBAND, A TENDER FATHER.
HE LIVED AND DIED A GOOD AND FAITHFUL
MASON AND ODD FELLOW
THE STORMS THAT WRECK THE WINTRY SKY,
NO MORE DISTURB THY DEEP REPOSE,
THAN SUMMER EVENING'S LATEST SIGH,
THAT SHUTS THE ROSE.
(RC-40)

BENEATH THIS TOMB IS DEPOSITED
THE REMAINS OF
HENRY GUYTON SMITH
WHO WAS BORN JULY 17th 1790
AND DIED SEPTEMBER 28th 1820

OH HUSBAND DARLING OF MY HEART,
HOW SOON WARE WE OBLIGED TO PART,
HOW EASILY DID DEATH DESTROY,
MY FONDEST HOPE MY DEAREST JOY,
BUT AS GOD SUMMONED THEE FROM HENCE,
I WILL SUBMIT TO PROVIDENCE.
REST THEN IN PEACE I WON'T COMPLAIN,
IN PARADISE WE WILL MEET AGAIN.
(RC-27)

SARAH ELIZABETH
ARTHUR
WIFE OF J. A. MOORE.
1819 - 1902.

"SO FADES A SUMMER CLOUD AWAY.
SO SINKS THE GALE WHEN
STORMS ARE O'ER.
SO GENTLY SHUTS THE EYE OF DAY.
SO DIES A WAVE ALONG
THE SHORE."
(RC-26)

IN THE MORNING OF LIFE
FROM A SCENE THEN FAIR WITH HOPE
BUT NOW IN HIS BEREAVEMENT
BY A MYSTERIOUS BUT WISE
PROVIDENCE OF GOD.
ALAS HOW CHANGED
JAMES LOUIS PETIGRU, JUN.
DROWNED IN THE LITTLE RIVER
LEFT TO HIS PARENTS
SUCH SOURCE OF GRIEF
AS IS ONLY KNOWN TO THOSE
WHO READ THE TOMB
TO AS ON THAT DESERVED THEIR LOVE
AND THAT OF AN ONLY SISTER
NAT. 11 JAN. 1832 ------- OBT. 12 SEPT. 1853
(MC-3)

JANE
WIFE OF
HENRY MILAM
DIED
OCT. 22, 1821
AGED ABOUT 55 YEARS
SHE PASSED BEYOND ALL
EARTHLY WOES
SHE SMILES IN A SUNNIER
SPHERE
(LR-1)

HERE
IS INTERRED
ALL THAT WAS MORTAL
OF
MRS. ELIZA TRALL DANIEL
SHE WAS LOVELY TO SOUL AND TO EYE
OB. 17 JULY A.D. 1819
AGE 27
CHISLEY DANIEL
DEDICATED THIS MONUMENT
TO HER MEMORY.
A TOKEN IF A HUSBAND'S
LOVE
(PK-3)

SARAH ELLEN
BELOVED WIFE OF JOHN R. HARRISON
1917 - 1964
* "SHE WALKED IN BEAUTY"
(AB-10)

*Though not original, it's beautiful for an epitaph.

TO THE MEMORY OF
MRS. MARY WELSH
WHO DEPARTED THIS LIFE
AUG 31ST 1799
AGED 23 YEARS & 5 MONTHS

WHAT CAN i ADD
FOR ALL MY WORDS ARE FAINT?
CELESTIAL LOVE
NO ELOQUENCE CAN PAINT.
NO MORE CAN BE
IN MORTAL WORDS EXPRESS'D,
BUT VAST ETERNITY
SHALL TELL THE REST.
(CT-60)

MARY E. LEE
"MY SISTER, AS SOME MIGHTY SWELL
DOTH PART TWO VESSELS TO ONE HAVEN BOUND,
SO DEATH HAS COME BETWEEN US!"
(CT-63)

SARAH L. SMITH
WIFE OF
W. JOEL SMITH,
BORN FEB. 17, 1835
DIED APR. 8, 1904
"SHE OPENED HER MOUTH WITH
WISDOM AND HER TONGUE WAS
THE LAW OF KINDNESS."
(AB-11)

IN MEMORY OF
FREDERICK BERDINE
BRUNSWICK, IN NEW JERSEY,
WHO DEPARTED THIS LIFE
AUGUST THE 18TH 1794
AGED 19 YEARS
ALAS! DEAR YOUTH, WE MUST THY FATE DEPLORE,
THUS DOOMED TO FALL FAR FROM THY NATIVE
SHORE;
BUT WHY REPINE? 'TWAS HEAVEN'S WILL' 'TIS BEST;
WE HOPE HE'S HAPPY NOW AMONGST THE BLEST.
(CT-59)

DIED
ON THE 3rd FEB. 1858
(???????) F. GRAVES
IN THE 31 YEAR OF HER AGE
"EARLY, BRIGHT, TRANSIENT,
CHASTE AS MORNING DEW,
SHE SPARKLED, WAS EXHAL-
TED AND WENT TO HEAVEN.
(AB-15)

MRS. RACHEL MARY
BARBER
DIED, MAY 14TH 1857,
IN THE 45 YEAR
OF HER AGE
"TO KNOW HER IS TO LOVE HER"
BURY ME THERE IN THAT CHURCH YARD OLD,
WHERE FLOWERS GIVE OUT THEIR SWEETS,
AND THE SABBATH BELL SO OFT HATH TOLLED,
FOR PASTOR AND FLOCK TO MEET.
'TIS DONE.
(CT-65)

CHAPTER 4

A SOLDIER'S TALE

Go tell the Spartans, stranger passing by,
that here, obedient to their law, we lie.

From the Poet Simonides of Ceos
for those lost at the battle of Thermopylae

THE HAYES STATION MASSACRE

The episode occurred at the end of the Revolutionary war on November 17, 1781 when the Tory Col. "Bloody" Bill Cunningham and three hundred of his men reached a militia station commanded by Militia Col. Joseph Hayes. The "Hayes Station" was nothing more than a blacksmith shop with with about two dozen S.C. Militiamen assembled to protect the women and children gathered inside. Cunningham and his men set fire to the shop forcing Col. Hayes and his men to surrender. Once outside the women and children were separated and forced to watch "Bloody Bill" and his men hack the militia to death with their sabers. The following Soldier is reputed to be the only one of Hayes' men to survive the ordeal.

IN
MEMORY OF
WM. BLAKELY, SR.
WHO WAS BORN
MAY 12th 1760
AND DEPARTED THIS LIFE
MAY 12th
1847

WILLIAM BLAKELY, SR.
PVT. CONTINENTAL LINE
REVOLUTIONARY WAR
MAY 12, 1760 - MAY 12, 1847
(LR-2)

THE WAXAW MASSACRE

The Battle of Waxhaw (a/k/a "Waxaw Massacre" or "Buford Massacre") began as a rather small skirmish when Sir Banastre Tarleton' (Col. of the Green Dragoon at the time) overtook Col Abraham Buford's Virginia Continentals. Overwhelmed at first, Buford refused to surrender or even stop marching. Tarleton and his men, a smaller but superior force, ruthlessly attacked Buford's men as they kept marching and only after sustaining heavy casualties did Buford finally surrender.

British and American accounts differ, but according to American observers, Tarleton and his men ignored the white flag and massacred Buford's men, eventually killing 113 and severely wounding 203, many of whom were so badly wounded they were left behind. Tarleton's casualties were minor with only 5 killed and 12 wounded. The battle and subsequent massacre earned Col. Tarleton the nickname "Bloody Ban" and "the Butcher."

The battle marked a turning point in the war by convincing those colonists who were neutral to join the rallying cry for American Patriots and independence. The phrase "Tarleton's Quarter" became a call for American Patriots to offer no quarter to British Soldiers or Loyalist and an end to "civilized warfare." The following monument is for those who died at the hands of Tarlton's men.

Left side:

ERECTED
TO THE MEMORY
AND HONOR OF
THE BRAVE AND PATRIOTIC
AMERICAN SOLDIERS,
WHO FELL IN BATTLE
WHICH OCCURRED AT THIS
PLACE ON THE 29TH
OF MAY 1780, BETWEEN
COL. ABRAHAM BUFORD
WHO COMMANDED A REGIMENT
OF 350 VIRGINIANS
AND COL. TARLETON
OF THE BRITISH ARMS
WITH 350 CALVARY AND A
LIKE NUMBER OF INFANTRY

Front side:

NEARLY
THE ENTIRE COMMAND
OF COL. BUFORD WERE
EITHER KILLED OR WOUNDED
GALLANT SOLDIERS ARE
BURIED IN THIS GRAVE
THEY LEFT THEIR HOMES
FOR THE RELIEF OF
CHARLESTON
HEARING AT CAMDEN
OF THE SURRENDER OF
THAT CITY
WERE RETURNING.
HERE THEIR LIVES WERE
ENDED IN THE SERVICE
OF THEIR COUNTRY

Right side:
THE CRUELTY
AND BARBAROUS MASSACRE
COMMITTED
ON THIS OCCASION
BY TARLETON AND HIS
COMMAND AFTER THE
SURRENDER OF COL. BUFORD
AND HIS REGIMENT
ORIGINATED
THE AMERICAN WAR CRY
"REMEMBER TARLETON'S
QUARTERS"
A BRITISH HISTORIAN
CONFESSES AT THIS BATTLE
THE VIRTUE OF HUMANITY
WAS TOTALLY FORGOT.
(LC-1)

THE EXECUTION OF ISAAC HAYNE

Col. Isaac Hayne was captured by the British and put on trial for violating his parole "to not take up arms against the British Crown". To set an example and strike fear in the hearts of the discontented Colonist, he was executed. This "example" of British brutality backfired, angering Colonist, inciting riots and causing many to enlist in the militia, swelling the ranks almost overnight.

COLONEL ISAAC HAYNE
PATRIOT - SOLDIER - MARTYR
BORN SEPTEMBER 23, 1745
MARRIED ELIZABETH HUTSON
JULY 18, 1765
WAS EXECUTED BY THE BRITISH CONTRARY
TO ALL USAGE'S OF WAR
AUG. 4, 1781
IN LIFE A SOLDIER OF HIS COUNTRY
IN DEATH A MARTYR TO HER SACRED CAUSE
HIS MEMORY AN UNDYING INSPIRATION TO
HIS FELLOW COUNTRYMEN,
HIS MONUMENT THE FREEDOM OF HIS LAND.
(CL-1)

THE EXECUTION OF CALVIN S. CROZIER

The following epitaph tells the story of a soldier who became something of a hero in Newberry, S.C.

Front side:

CALVIN S. CROZIER
BORN
AT BRANDON, MISS.,
AUGUST 1840,
MURDERED
AT NEWBERRY, S. C.
SEPT. 8, 1865

Right side:

AFTER THE SURRENDER OF THE
CONFEDERATE ARMIES, WHILE ON
THE WAY TO HIS HOME IN TEXAS
FROM A FEDERAL PRISON HE
WAS CALLED UPON AT THE
RAILROAD STATION AT
NEWBERRY, S. C., ON THE NIGHT
OF SEPT. 7, 1865,
TO PROTECT A YOUNG WHITE
WOMAN TEMPORARILY
UNDER HIS CHARGE FROM GROSS
INSULTS OFFERED BY A NEGRO
FEDERAL SOLDIER OF THE
GARRISON STATIONED THERE

Rear side:

A DIFFICULTY ENSUED IN WHICH
THE NEGRO WAS SLIGHTLY CUT
THE INFURIATED SOLDIERS
SEIZED A CITIZEN OF NEWBERRY
UPON WHOM
THEY WERE ABOUT TO EXECUTE
SAVAGE REVENGE,

WHEN CROZIER CAME PROMPTLY
FORWARD AND AVOWED HIS OWN
RESPONSIBILITY FOR THE DEED,
THUS REFUSING TO ACCEPT SAFETY
FROM ALLOWING A STRANGER
TO RECEIVE THE VIOLENCE
INTENDED FOR HIMSELF.

Top left side:

HE WAS HURRIED IN THE
NIGHT TIME TO THE
BIVOUAC OF THE REGIMENT TO
WHICH THE SOLDIER BELONGED,
WAS KEPT UNDER GUARD
ALL NIGHT, WAS NOT
ALLOWED COMMUNICATION WITH
ANY CITIZEN, WAS CONDEMNED
TO DIE WITHOUT EVEN THE
FORM OF A TRIAL AND
WAS SHOT TO DEATH
ABOUT DAY LIGHT THE
FOLLOWING MORNING AND
HIS BODY MUTILATED.

Bottom left side:

REST ON, EMBALMED AND SAINTED DEAD,
DEAR AS THE BLOOD YOU GAVE.
NO IMPIOUS FOOTSTEPS HERE SHALL TREAD,
THE HERBAGE OF YOUR GRAVE,
NOR SHALL YOUR GLORY BE FORGOT.
WHILE FAME HER RECORD KEEPS,
OR HONOR POINTS THE HALLOWED SPOT,
WHERE VALOR PROUDLY SLEEPS.

(NB-4)

69

UNION ARMY WOMAN

The first American Woman to ever be buried in a national military cemetery lies near the site of the Florence Stockade, a former Confederate Prison Camp. Florena Budwin, posing as a man, enlisted in the Union Army with her husband. The two were captured in late 1864 and sent to the notorious Andersonville prison camp where he died and she was soon transferred to the Florence Stockade. Florena's gender was only discovered after an epidemic struck the prison camp and she was forced to see a Confederate doctor. She died soon after and is buried near the trench graves of over 2,000 of her fellow Union POW's who died in camp of disease and starvation.

FLORENA BUDWIN
JAN 25, 1865
(FL-2)

TO THE MEMORY OF
PVT. WILLIAM J. KING
HUSBAND OF JANE C. KING
B. - 1823 --- D. - AUGUST 23, 1863
IN THE SERVICE OF C.S.A.
CAPT. GEO. COX'S CO.
ORR'S RIFLE REG.

TO WM. K. :
"WHEN THIS YOU SEE REMEMBER
ME THO MANY MILE APART
WILL BE"
J.C.K.
INTERRED:
OAKWOOD NATL. CEM.
RICHMOND VA.
(AB-12)

RICHARD KIRKLAND
C.S.A.
WHO AT THE BATTLE OF FREDRICKSBURG RISKED HIS
LIFE TO CARRY WATER TO WOUNDED AND DYING
ENEMIES
AND AT THE BATTLE OF CHICKAMAUGA LAID
DOWN HIS LIFE FOR HIS COUNTRY
1843 – 1863
"IF THINE ENEMY THIRST GIVE HIM DRINK"
(KS-1)

JOSEPH H. GASSAWAY
A PALMETTO SOLDIER
DIED 1848
(EF-5)

71

JUDGE E. BROWN
SON OF
JAMES C. & ELIZABETH A.
BROWN
BORN JULY 10, 1849
DIED IN
THE N. Y. HOSPITAL
AUG. 8, 1865
TAKEN PRISONER BY
SHERMAN'S TROOPS
(BW-1)

HERE REST
ALL THAT IS MORTAL
OF
ROBERT MARTIN
LT. COLONEL, C. S. A.
BORN IN CHARLESTON, S. C.
FEBRUARY 12th, 1835,
DIED IN AUGUSTA GA.
MAY 24th, 1874
A LOYAL GENTLEMAN
A DEVOTED PATRIOT
A SINCERE CHRISTIAN
TO A LOFTY COURAGE
AND RARE CIVIC VIRTUE
HE ADDED THE CHARMS
OF NOBLE MANNERS
AND HIGH ACCOMPLISHMENT
STEADFAST AMID THE FIRECAST
CONVULSIONS OF THE CIVIL WAR
AND BY IT'S TEMPTATIONS AND
CORRUPTIONS UNSEDUCED
(AL3)

HERE LIE THE BODIES OF
LIEUT.
WILLIAM CALDERWOOD
AND ENSIGN JOHN FINLEY
OF COL. PREVOST BRITISH
TROOPS KILLED IN BATTLE NEAR
GRAY'S HILL FEB. 3, 1779
BURIED HERE FEB. 5, 1779
REST IN PEACE
(BF-1)

IN MEMORY OF
LIEUT. JAMES WILLIS CANTEY
OF THE PALMETTO REGIMENT
SON OF
JAMES WILLIS AND
CAMILLA RICHARDSON CANTEY
BORN NOV. 21, 1822
DIED IN THE FIELD OF BATTLE
SEPT. 13, 1847

ON THE 13th SEPT. 1847,
THE CASTLE OF CHAPULTEPEC,
WAS CARRIED BY STORM,
WHILE LEADING HIS MEN TO A BREACH
IN THE WALLS WHICH HE HAD DISCOVERED,
THIS GALLANT SOLDIER
FELL BEFORE IT, SHOT IN THE FRONT,
AND DIED UNDER THE VICTORIOUS
FLAG OF HIS COUNTRY.
"HOW SLEEP THE BRAVE WHO SINK TO REST,
BY ALL THEIR COUNTRY'S WISHES BLEST."
(KS-2)

WHITFORD BUTLER
BROOKS
CO. B. 6, S. C.
21, JULY 1845
12, JUNE 1864
KILLED BATTLE
TREVILLIAN, Va.
BRIEF YET BRAVE
AND GLORIOUS WAS
HIS YOUNG CAREER.
(EF-6)

ACT'G LT. HAMBLETON F. PORTER
U.S. NAVY
FOURTH SON OF THE LATE
COMM'D DAVID PORTER
DIED 11TH AUGUST 1844
AGED 24 YEARS
THIS SLAB IS RESPECTFULLY DEDICATED
TO HIS MEMORY
BY HIS SHIPMATES
THE OFFICERS AND CREW
OF THE U.S. SCHOONER FLIRT
(CT-33)

BRIG. GEN.
MILLAGE L. BONHAM
ARMY OF
THE POTOMAC
C.S.A.
DEC. 25 1813
AUG. 27 1890
(RC-11)

TO THE MEMORY
OF COL. ANDREW
PICKENS, SR.
C. 1690 – 1756
AND WIFE
ANN DAVIS
PICKENS
PARENTS OF GEN.
ANDREW PICKENS
HERO OF THE
REVOLUTIONS
(LC-5)

GEO. ADDISON
BORN
28TH FEBRUARY 1833
DIED
2ND FEBRUARY 1876
WAS AN OFFICER
ON THE ALABAMA
SAVED THE PAPERS
OF THE SHIP
AND DELIVERED
THEM TO
CAPT. SEMMES
(CT-98)

JOHN MAJORIBANKS, Esq.
LATE MAJOR TO THE 19th Regt. Inf.
AND COMMANDING A FLANK Bat.
OF HIS MAJESTY'S ARMY Obiit.
22d of Octr. 1781
(OB-1)

SAMPLE
WILLIAM LESLIE SAMPLE
JAN. 11, 1901,
AUG. 21, 1918.
BUT A LAD OF 17 YEARS, HE VOLUNTEERED
AND GAVE HIS LIFE FOR HIS COUNTRY.
(NB-3)

TO
THE MEMORY OF
CAPTAIN JAMES DAVIS
WHO SERVED OUR
REPUBLIC AS A
FAITHFUL SOLDIER
AND OFFICER
DURING THE
REVOLUTIONARY WAR
AND CONTINUED
A FIRM PATRIOT
TO HIS DEATH IN
1822
AGED 68 YEARS
(FF-8)

ROBERT C. KERR
ENSIGN NAVAL AIR CORPS
DIED OCT. 24, 1944
BATTLE OF "LEYTE",
AWARDED NAVY CROSS
POSTHUMOUSLY
BURIED AT SEA
(CT-99)

CAPT. S. M. ROOF
1830 - 1919
PATRIOTIC
CITIZEN
HEROIC
CONFEDERATE
SOLDIER
1861 - 1865
COMING IS THE DAY
AND FAST, WHEN ON
MARBLE SHALL BE READ:
"THE GALLANT GRAYS HAVE PASSED."
(LX-1)

IN MEMORY
OF MY BELOVED BROTHER
HARMON FREDERICK,
SON OF CHAS. & SARAH NEUFFER,
BORN 24th DEC. 1836,
DIED 11th AUGUST 1861.
HE WAS A MEMBER OF THE
"COLUMBIA GREYS"
2nd REGT. S. C. V. AND DIED IN THE
SERVICE OF HIS COUNTRY
NEAR VIENNA, VIRGINIA.

YES MY DARLING BROTHER THOU ART GONE,
TO THAT BRIGHT AND HAPPY HOME.
IN HEAVEN WHERE WARS AND TUMULTS CEASE,
WHERE FOES ARE NOT, BUT ALL IS PEACE;
WHERE WE SHALL MEET THE LOVED ONES GONE
BEFORE,
THERE ARE NO TEARS AND PARTINGS COME NO MORE.
SALLIE C. NEUFFER
(RC-8)

TO THE MEMORY
OF
LIEUT. EDWARD WALLACE
YOUNGEST SON OF
ANDREW AND SARAH WALLACE

FOR TWO YEARS A SOLDIER WHO FOUGHT IN
MANY BATTLE FIELDS WITH DISTINGUISHED
BRAVERY. BORN IN COLUMBIA So. Ca.
FEBRUARY 24th, 1838. DIED APRIL 9th, 1863
IN RICHMOND VIRGINIA, FROM DISEASE
CONTRACTED IN CAMP NEAR FREDRICKSBURG.
HE WAS POSSESSED OF TRUE COURAGE,
AN AMIABLE NATURE,
COMBINED WITH STRONG INTELLECT
AND HIGH MORAL
CHARACTER.
(RC-9)

GENERAL WILLIAM OSWALD
DIED NOVEMBER 12th 1825
AGED 48 YEARS; 1 MONTH;
4 DAYS.

THE MAN WHO MAKES FROM DAY TO DAY
IN GENEROUS ACTS HIS RADIANT WAY,
TREADS THE SAME PATH HIS SAVIOR TROD
THE PATH TO GLORY AND TO GOD.
(CL-3)

THE DUST
OF
DR. JAMES DAVIS
1st SURGEON OF THE
PALMETTO REGIMENT.
BELIEVING THE DUTIES OF LIFE
TO BE GREATER THAN LIFE ITSELF
HE SACRIFICED HIS HEALTH IN
THEIR ARDUOUS PERFORMANCE
TO HIS REGIMENT IN MEXICO
AND DIED SOON AFTER HE RETURNED
TO HIS HOME AND NATIVE
PLACE COLUMBIA
APRIL 23rd 1818
AGED 27
(RC-39)

Front side:

JOHN
CALVERT LIEUTENANT
S.C. MILITIA
REV. WAR
1734 - 1803

Back side:

AT THE
LIBERTY TREE
CHARLESTON
1766
HE PLEDGED
TO RESIST
BRITISH TAXATION
(RC-35)

ERECTED
BY A SORROWING MOTHER
TO THE MEMORY OF
HER BELOVED SON
JACOB BLANKENSTEIN
WHO WAS BORN JULY 28th 1841,
FELL ON THE 2nd OF MAY 1863, AT
THE BATTLE OF CHANCELLORVILLE, VA.

HIS DAYS HOW SHORT, HOW EARLY CALLED AWAY,
TO PAY THAT DEBT, EACH MORTAL HAS TO PAY,
BUT CEASE TO MORN YE FRIEND FROM TEARS
REFRAIN,
OUR TRANSIENT LOSS, IS HIS ETERNAL GAIN.
(RC-41)

IN MEMORY OF
SERGT. CHARLES E. FLYNN
BORN IN COLA, S. C.
APRIL 4th 1814,
FELL ON THE BATTLE FIELD OF
CHICKAMAUGA,
SEPT. 20th 1863,
WHILST CHEERING HIS COMRADES
TO VICTORY OR DEATH.

FIRM AS THE FIRMEST WHERE DUTY LED,
HE HURRIED WITHOUT A FALTER,
BOLD AS THE BOLDEST HE FOUGHT AND BLED,
AND THE DAY WAS WON BUT THE FIELD WAS RED,
AND THE BLOOD
OF THE FRESH YOUNG HEART WAS SHED,
ON HIS COUNTRY'S HALLOWED ALTER.
REQUIESCAT IN PEACE. AMEN
(RC-42)

IN THE MEMORY OF
MAJ. JAMES ALSTON
BORN
NOVEMBER 16, 1774
DIED
DECEMBER 15, 1850
AN OFFICER
IN THE SEMINOLE WAR,
HE SERVED HIS COUNTRY
WITH ZEAL, COURAGE
AND EFFICIENCY

THE PATRIOTIC CITIZEN.
THE MAN OF HONOR AND TRUTH.
THE FAITHFUL FRIEND.
THE TENDER AND DEVOTED
HUSBAND AND FATHER.
(AB-5)

THIS MARBLE
IS ERECTED TO THE MEMORY OF
LIEUT. RUSSEL BASSKETT,
LATE COMMANDER OF THE
UNITED STATES SCHOONER
ALLIGATOR
BY HIS BROTHER OFFICERS,
AS A MARK OF THEIR ESTEEM
HE WAS BORN IN THE COUNTY OF
DERBY, STATE OF CONNECTICUT,
ON THE 23D OF JANUARY, 1784,
AND DIED OF A FEVER IN THIS
CITY, ON THE 3RD OF SEP. 1814
AGED 30 YRS, 7 MONTHS, 11 DAYS
(CT-72)

SACRED TO THE MEMORY
OF HENRY BRADLEY WHO
DEPARTED THIS LIFE ON THE 8TH OF APRIL
A.D. 1825
AGED FORTY THREE YEARS
HE LONG ENJOYED THE CONFIDENCE AND
RESPECT OF HIS FELLOW CITIZENS
AND WAS BY THEM
ADVANCED TO EVERY OFFICE IN THEIR GIFT FOR
WHICH HE WAS A CANDIDATE
AT THE TIME OF HIS DISEASE HE WAS MAJOR
GENERAL COMMANDING THE THIRD DIVISION
OF SOUTH CAROLINA MILITIA, CONSISTING OF
EIGHT REGIMENTS OF INFANTRY, TWO REGIMENTS
OF CALVARY, BESIDES ARTILLERY AND RIFLEMEN
HIS TERM OF SERVICE AS LIEUTENANT GOVERNOR OF
THIS STATE HAD BUT A SHORT TIME EXPIRED AT HIS
DISEASE, IN HIM SOCIETY HAS LOST A USEFUL
MEMBER
AND TO HIS BEREAVED FRIENDS HIS LOSS IS
IRREPARABLE
(CS-13)

VICTOR BLUE
*REAR ADMIRAL U.S. NAVY
DEC 6, 1865
JAN. 22 1928
V.B.
HOME IS THE SAILOR
HOME FROM THE SEA
(MR-1)

*Admiral Blue was a veteran of the Spanish American War and the Boxer Rebellion in China in command of the Pacific Fleet.

IN MEMORY OF
LIEUT. JOSEPH FRIEDEBERG.
OF THE HARPER RIFLES
JAMES BATTALION, S. C. V.
WHO WAS BORN IN CHARLESTON, S. C.
ON THE 11th OF AUGUST, 1823
AND DIED AT MIDDLETOWN, MD.
IN THE HANDS OF THE ENEMY,
ON THE 18th OF SEPTEMBER, 1862,
FROM EFFECTS OF WOUNDS
RECEIVED AT THE
BATTLE OF BOONSBORO.
(RC-7)

IN MEMORY OF
JAMES HOLT GREEN
SON OF
DAISIE HOLT AND WALTER GUERRY GREEN
LIEUTENANT UNITED STATES NAVEL RESERVE
BORN IN CHARLESTON S.C. OCTOBER 8, 1909
KILLED BY THE ENEMY AT MAUTHAUSEN IN
GERMAN OCCUPIED AUSTRIA,
JANUARY 26, 1945, AS A RESULT OF A VOLUNTARY
MISSION BEHIND ENEMY LINES IN CZECHOSLOVAKIA
DISTINGUISHED SERVICE CROSS,
CZECHOSLOVAK WAR CROSS
(CT-101)

THOMAS M. SEAL
MUS.
2 S.C. INF.
SP'AM WAR
(AB-14)

GEN. ANDREW PICKENS
WAS BORN
13th SEPTEMBER 1739
AND DIED
11th AUGUST 1817
HE WAS A CHRISTIAN
A PATRIOT & SOLDIER
HIS CHARACTER & ACTIONS
ARE INCORPORATED WITH THE
HISTORY OF THIS COUNTRY
FILIAL AFFECTION & RESPECT
RAISE THIS STONE
TO HIS MEMORY
(PK-7)

SACRED
TO THE MEMORY OF
GENERAL PETER HORRY
WHO LEFT THIS MORTAL LIFE ON THE
28th DAY OF FEBRUARY, A.D. 1815
AGED ABOUT 68 YEARS
HE DISPLAYED A CONSPICUOUS
CHARACTER AS AN OFFICER
IN THE AMERICAN
REVOLUTIONARY WAR
(RC-57)

MARK WAYNE CLARK
1896 – 1984
GENERAL U.S. ARMY
PRESIDENT OF THE CITADEL
1954 – 1965
(CT-2)

SACRED
TO THE MEMORY OF
THOMAS PETIGRU,
U.S.N. COMMANDER
BORN 1ST JUNE 1793,
DIED 6TH MARCH 1857

COURAGE FEELING AND TRUTH
MARKED HIS COURSE.
IN THE NAVAL SERVICE HE ENFORCED
THE WHOLESOME LAWS OF DISCIPLINE
AND IN PRIVATE LIFE EXTENDED
THE OPEN HAND OF CHARITY
HE LOVED JUSTICE AND MADE THE
OFFENDER BOW TO ITS MANDATE
AND WAS THEREFORE PERSECUTED AND
VINDICATED IN THE FACE OF DAY
HE WAS WOUNDED IN THE DARK
AND DIED AT HIS POST
DEMANDING REPARATION.

CLOUDS OBSCURE THE EVENING
OF HIS DAY
AND HE BORE THE HARDEST TRIALS
WITHOUT DESCENDING FROM THE
ELEVATION OF MANLY CHARACTER.
FRIENDSHIP MOURNED BY HIS
DYING BED.
NOR WILL THE SENSE OF THEIR LOSS
DEPART BUT WITH LIFE
FROM THE BOSOM OF THEM WHO WITH
CONJUGAL AND FRATERNAL AFFECTION
DRESS THIS TOMB TO HIS MEMORY.
(M2-2)

IN MEMORY
OF
JAMES SAMUEL WILSON
SON OF CAPT. J. R. WILSON
WHO WAS BORN SEPTEMBER 5th 1841
NEAR DUE WEST, ABBEVILLE DISTRICT.

WHEN THE WAR COMMENCED FOR SOUTHERN
RIGHTS AND INDEPENDENCE HE WAS A STUDENT
AT ERSKINE COLLEGE, A MEMBER OF THE JUNIOR
CLASS,
AND ALTHOUGH OF SLENDER AND DELICATE FRAME,
HE
HESITATED NOT WHEN HIS COUNTRY WAS IN DANGER.
IN FEB. 1861, HE VOLUNTEERED & UNITED WITH
COMP'Y "B"
7th S. C. REG. WITH WHICH HE REMAINED UP TO FEB.
1862 WHEN HE WAS SEVERELY ATTACKED WITH
RHEUMATISM.

IN APRIL HE WAS DISCHARGED AND SENT HOME ON
CRUTCHES. IN OCT'R HE UNITED WITH THE PRES'B
CHURCH AT LONG CANE AND IN MARCH 1863 WHEN
ONLY PARTIALLY RECOVERED FROM HIS
RHEUMATIC AFFECTION WITH WEAK AND STIFFENED
JOINTS HE AGAIN RETURNED TO THE SERVICE OF HIS
COUNTRY, UNITED WITH COMP'Y "G" ORR'S REGIMENT
AND ON SUNDAY THE 3rd OF MAY 1863 WHILE IN THE
CHARGE AT CHANCELERSVILLE VA.

HE FELL PIERCED IN THE LEFT BREAST WITH A MINNIE
BALL AND DIED WITHOUT A STRUGGLE.
(AB-13)

86

CHAPTER 5
FIRST RIGHTS &
CLAIMS

Truth and History.
21 Men. The Boy Bandit King.
He Died As He Lived
William H. Bonney "Billy the Kid"

The Epitaph of William H. Bonney

THE CHARGE OF THE LIGHT BRIGADE

Below lies the epitaph of John H.L. Fuller, a British soldier who was assigned to the Light Brigade of the British Calvary during the Crimean War. Because of a miscommunication his unit of over six hundred were told to charge toward the heavily armed Russian army without support from the Heavy Brigade and other forces. The Light Brigade took fire from three sides resulting in about two hundred and fifty men killed along with most of the horses in less than twenty minutes.

Their charge was immortalized in Alfred Lord Tennyson's poem, "Charge of the Light Brigade." Fuller's epitaph states that "he" is the only survivor to be buried in America.

SACRED
TO THE MEMORY OF
MY BELOVED HUSBAND
*JOHN H. L. FULLER
WHO DIED IN THIS CITY
SEPTEMBER 6TH 1871
IN THE 38 YEAR OF HIS AGE

THE ONLY MEMBER OF THE GALLANT 600
THAT CHARGED AT BALAKLAVA RUSSIA
BURIED IN AMERICA
(CT-102)

Or was he??? Read on.....

WILLIAM HENRY CORY
BORN IN CLAPHAM ENGLAND
MAY 2, 1831
SURVIVOR OF THE FAMOUS CHARGE
OF THE LIGHT BRIGADE AT
BALACLAVE, OCT. 25, 1854
SERVED IN CONFEDERATE ARMY
1862 - 1865
DIED JAN. 29, 1893
(BF-2)

"A WOMAN OF THE REVOLUTION"

Tradition has it that Mary (Gill) Mills assisted her brother, Robert Gill, in making several swords for General Sumter during the Revolutionary War. The swords never made it to the troops. Gill was captured by the British in route with his delivery.

TO
THE MEMORY OF
COL. JOHN MILLS
WHO DIED
MARCH 19TH 1795
IN THE 38TH YEAR OF
HIS AGE
THIS MONUMENT IS DEDICATED BY
HIS AFFECTIONATE CHILDREN

HERE
ALSO REPOSE
THE MORTAL REMAINS OF HIS CONSORT
MRS. MARY MILLS
BORN OCTOBER 1758 IN THE COLONY OF
PENNSYLVANIA
DIED JAN'Y 29TH 1841 IN THE STATE OF SOUTH
CAROLINA IN THE 84TH YEAR OF HER AGE
A WOMAN OF THE REVOLUTION, SHE POSSESSED
IN AN EMINENT DEGREE, THOSE STERLING QUALITIES
WHICH PROVED SUPERIOR TO THE EMERGENCIES
WHICH CALLED HER FORTH AND FITTED HER TO BE
A BLESSING TO THE COUNTRY IN THE HOUR OF HER
COUNTRIES NEED
SHE DIED IN THE COMMUNION OF FISHING CREEK
CHURCH
(CS-20)

GARY'S BATTLES

While Brigadier General Martin W. Gary served in many battles as listed on his headstone, he also fought many more battles as a radical Democrat and violent racist. Under the "Edgefield Plan" Gary and his "Red Shirts" had an injurious influence in shaping post re-construction South Carolina politics.

MARTIN W. GARY
MAR 10, 1831
APRIL 9, 1881
C.S.A.
CAPTAIN, LIEUTENANT COLONEL,
COLONEL, BRIGADIER GENERAL,
MAJOR GENERAL
MANASSAS, ELKORN'S LANDING,
SEVEN PINES, CAINE'S MILL,
MALVERN HILL, SECOND MANASSAS,
CHANTILLY, BOONESBORO GAP
SHARPSBURG, FREDERICKSBURG,
SUFFOLK, WILLS VALLEY,
CAMPBELL'S STATION, KNOXVILLE,
BEAN'S STATION, MAFODAQUEEN
CREEK, RIDDLE'S SHOP,
SYMMONIA CHURCH, TILGHMAN'S
CAPE, FUSSELL'S MILL, NEW MARKET
HEIGHTS, LAUREL HILL CHURCH,
DARBYTOWN, WILLIAMSBURG ROAD,
NINE MILE ROAD, AMELIA SPRING,
APPOMATTOX, C.H.
JURIST, PATRIOT, HERO,
STATESMAN
(GW-2)

JNO. MONTAGUE.
U. S. SOLDIER. REV. WAR.
DIED SEPT. 20, 1831
AGED 80 YEARS.

HE RECEIVED A SABER WOUND
ON HIS HEAD AND ARM WHILE
DEFENDING GEN. WASHINGTON
AGAINST A BRITISH OFFICER.
(GW-1)

SACRED
TO THE MEMORY OF
MAJOR ANDREW HAMILTON
WHO DEPARTED THIS LIFE
ON THE 17th OF JANUARY 1835
IN THE 95th YEAR
OF HIS AGE

----

*THE NAME OF MAJOR HAMILTON
IS CONNECTED WITH ALMOST THE WHOLE
OF THE REVOLUTIONARY HISTORY
OF THE UP COUNTRY OF
SOUTH CAROLINA
HE DIED A MEMBER OF THE
PRESBYTERIAN CHURCH AND HIS
MEMORY IS REVERED BY MANY
KINDRED AND FRIENDS.
(AB-4)

*Not much is known or "connected" with the name Major Hamilton other than he fought in the Battle of Kettle Creek and served under General Andrew Pickens.

IN MEMORY OF
REVEREND SAMUEL THOMAS
OF
BALLYDON ENGLAND
1672 - 1706
FIRST MISSIONARY SENT TO SOUTH CAROLINA
BY THE SOCIETY FOR THE PROPAGATION OF THE
GOSPEL
IN FOREIGN PARTS.
(BK-4)

R.J. HANNA
SEPT. 3, 1880
OCT. 31, 1969
SURVIVOR
OF THE
TITANIC 1912
NEARER MY GOD
TO THEE
(BB-3)

SACRED
TO THE MEMORY OF
JOHN FRANCIS DALLOZ
BORN AT ST. GLAUDE FRANCE
IN THE YEAR 1788.
DEPARTED THIS LIFE IN THIS CITY *(COLUMBIA)*
NOV. 19, 1831
A SOLDIER UNDER NAPOLEON,
AND SEVERELY WOUNDED AT THE BATTLE OF
WATERLOO.
(RC-6)

WILLIAM MAXWELL
MARTIN
BORN 4th JUNE 1837
DIED 21st FEB. 1861
"THE FIRST MARTYR TO
SOUTHERN INDEPENDENCE."
HIS DEATH CAUSED
BY EXPOSURE IN DEFENSE
OF HIS NATIVE STATE
AT FORT MOULTRIE

"FURL OVER THE POET'S GRAVE
THE BANNER, THAT HE SANG,"
"AND LAY UPON HIS NARROW CELL
THE TUNEFUL LYRE HE LOVED SO WELL."
(RC-67)

WILLIAM MAULDIN
DIED AT 31
1873
FIRED FIRST CANNON
OF THE CIVIL WAR
AT FT. SUMTER
(PK-9)

SARAH WAYNE
GARDINER
1757 – 1821
WIFE OF McCALLA
HEROINE OF
THE REVOLUTION
(CS-4)

THE REMAINS OF
SAMUEL MATHIS,
SON OF
DANIEL AND SOPHIA MATHIS
BORN 22nd MARCH 1760,
DIED 26th SEPT. 1823,
AGED 63 YEARS, 6 MO, 4 DAYS.
THE DECEASED WAS THE FIRST WHITE PERSON
BORN IN CAMDEN. NATURALLY ACTIVE AND
ENTERPRISING, AND LIVING IN AN AGE OF
EXTRAORDINARY EVENTS AND REVOLUTION
HE PASSED THROUGH MANY CHEQUERED
EVENTS WHICH TAUGHT HIM THIS IMPORTANT
TRUTH, THAT ALL IS VANITY WHICH IS NOT HONEST
AND THAT THERE IS NO SOLID WISDOM BUT IN
REAL PIETY.
(KS-14)

*RUDOLH ANDERSON, JR.
MAJOR U.S. AIR FORCE
SEPTEMBER 15, 1927
OCTOBER 27, 1962
SON OF
RUDOLF AND MARY ANDERSON

KOREA
CUBAN MISSILE CRISIS
AIR FORCE CROSS

DSM DFC+20LC AM+10LC PH
KSM+1BSS NDSM+1BSS UNSM
(GV-3)
*Anderson was shot down over Cuba making him the ONLY
casualty during the Cuban Missile Crisis.

IN LOVING MEMORY OF
MY DEAR GRANDMOTHER
MRS. MARTHA MILNER PHILLIPS;
RELICT OF
ELEAZER PHILLIPS
A SOLDIER OF THE REVOLUTION
IN THOSE TRYING SCENES SHE
WAS HERSELF A WITNESS AND
HEROIC SUFFERER BEARING TO
HER GRAVE THE SCAR OF A WOUND
RECEIVED IN A BAYONET THRUST
WHEN ONLY 14 YEARS OLD WHILE
DEFENDING HER CHILD-BROTHER
FROM THE VIOLENCE OF A TORY
IN THE COMPANY OF CAPT. LUNDY
A BRITISH OFFICER.
BORN 10TH MAY 1765
DIED 17TH DEC 1856
"IN PEACE WITH GOD, IN CHARITY
WITH THE WORLD"
H.L.P.
(CT-58)

CHAPTER 6

PHOTOGRAPHS

A good snapshot stops a moment from running away.

Eudora Welty

A TOMB WITH A VIEW

Perhaps the strangest churchyards belongs to the Washington Street United Methodist Church in Columbia. It was mistakenly torched by Sherman's raiders who mistook it for the First Baptist Church, the site of the First Confederate Convention. When it came time to rebuild the church, the original location was found to be an unsuitable site, and the new church was constructed over a portion of the cemetery.

One of the graves under the church building belongs to Mrs. Sophia Nance. Sophia was so beautiful and adored by her husband, friends and family, she was buried in a metal sarcophagus with a glass window for viewing purposes. She can be found (with permission from the church) by entering a trap door in a broom closet and crawling under the building to her grave. Unfortunately, years ago the glass window cracked and mold has obscured her face.....but, the reader will be happy to know that pictures of Sophia before the glass was broken are located after her epitaph.

SOPHIA CATHARINE NANCE
CONSORT OF FREDck A. NANCE
BORN JULY 10, 1824
DIED JANUARY 24, 1853
(RC-65)

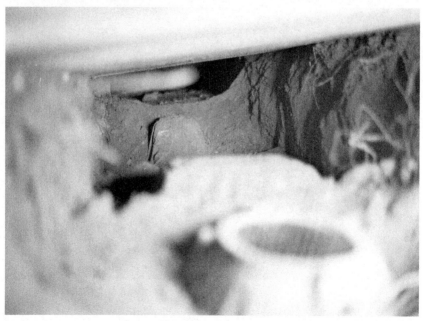

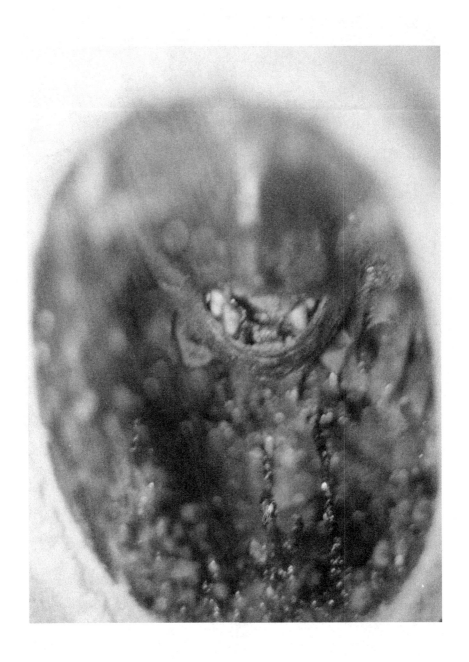

101

"SCARED" TO THE MEMORY OF
Even stone cutters make mistakes.

BABY'S CRIB PLANTER WITH BRONZE
Probably the most poignant cemetery monuments encountered. The bronze death mask seen up close is stunning. Located in a large family plot at Charleston's Magnolia Cemetery.

"THE LORD IS KIND"
Curious looking boy sitting on a chair.

GIRL WITH FLOWERS
Young girl holding flowers with melancholy expression.

LEPROSY STONE

This stone was brought from a leper colony in China founded by the interred as a personal monument.

THE GRAVE OF OSENAPPA

Traditional piled stones of a Cherokee Indian buried in a "white" cemetery about 1794. Little is known about this oddity.

THE GRAVE OF AGNES OF GLASGOW
Her journey to America for love is legendary. She was
alleged to have been buried by her Indian companion in the
dark of night.

MAGNOLIA CEMETERY, CHARLESTON, SC
This incomparable cemetery sits on a pristine estuary and is on the National Register of Historic Places. An eerily magical place.

"BUBBA" THE DOG

18TH CENTURY EFFIGIES FROM CHARLESTON, SC

THE SENTRY OF THE CEMETERY

A NYMPH OF WONDER

A PYRAMID TOMB

MATTY AND BOOTY

CHAPTER 7

WORK, WORK, WORK

"The Body of B. Franklin, printer
Like the Cover of an old Book
It's Contents torn out
And stripped of its Lettering & guilding
Lies here food for worms
For, it will as he believed appear once more
In a new and more elegant edition
Corrected and improved by the Author."

Epitaph of Benjamin Franklin

MUSICIANS, ACTORS & ARTIST

I'M WITH THE BAND

Interred at Greenlawn Memorial Gardens in Spartanburg , SC are half of the founding members of the *Marshal Tucker Band:* lead guitarist and vocalist Toy Caldwell, Jr. (1947-1993); his brother and bassist Tommy Caldwell (1949-1980); & rhythm guitarist George F. McCorkle (1947–2007). According to local stories, some can still hear their songs on the wind. Below is Tommy Caldwell's epitaph.

THOMAS
MICHAEL
CALDWELL
"TOMMY"
BORN NOVEMBER 9, 1949
TO
TOY & VIRGINIA CALDWELL
DEVOTED HUSBAND OF MELODY ANN HOPE
COMPOSER AND BASS GUITARIST
FOUNDER AND LEADER MARSHALL TUCKER BAND
VETERAN, UNITED STATES MARINE CORPS

ENTERED INTO ETERNAL LIFE
APRIL 28, 1980

"WITHOUT YOU THERE'LL NEVER BE NO SUNSHINE
WITHOUT YOU THERE'LL NEVER BE NO PRECIOUS RAIN
WHAT WOULD I DO IF YOU EVER UPT' AND LEFT ME
I'D START ALL OVER LOVING YOU AGAIN."
(SB-2)

KING OF THE PIEDMONT BLUES

Born in Laurens, SC as Pinkney Anderson, "Pink" joined Dr. Frank Kerr's *Indian Remedy Company* at the age of 14 as a performer. While honing his skills as a minstrel singer in medicine shows Pink soaked up ragtime, folk, and the Delta blues, reinterpreting them as Piedmont blues, of which he became the master. He recorded four songs in 1928, and again in the 1950s and '60s during the blues revival.

PINK ANDERSON
FEB. 12, 1900
OCT. 12, 1974
RECORDING ARTIST
(SB-1)

KING OF THE PIEDMONT BLUEGRASS

While not well know outside Bluegrass circles, Charlie Moore is a Bluegrass Legend, and part of the Piedmont musical history. Moore's singing style is from the Bill Monroe school of "lonesome" style of Mountain Bluegrass.

CHARLES B.
MOORE, JR
"CHARLIE"
1935 – 1979
"BLUEGRASS LEGEND"
(GV-6)

*BROOK BENTON
1932 – 1988
(KS-16)

*A strange epitaph on slab which looked like a pile of gravel with rubber letters placed on top. Benton was a singer and master song-writer, most famous for his song, *Rainy Night in Georgia*.

"RONNIE"
RONALD WAYNE
GARVIN
AUGUST 18, 1959
OCTOBER 7, 1996
THE WORLD HAS LOST A GREAT MUSICIAN
HIS MUSIC WILL BE FOREVER IN THE HEARTS
OF HIS FAMILY AND FANS
(CT-111)

*Garvin was guitarist for the band *Stranger* in the 1980's.

IN MEMORY OF MISS JANE WEIR
WHOSE SOUL IS FLED, HER DUST LIES HERE,
FIFTY FIVE YEARS, THAT'S NEAR HER AGE,
AND TIME SHE ACTED ON THE STAGE
IN VIRTUES PATH, SHE ALWAYS TROD
AND NOW IS GONE TO DWELL WITH GOD.
1811.
(MC-9)

JENNIE FERGUSON BACON
BORN JUNE 7, 1894
DIED JULY 28, 1939
WAS A GOSPEL SINGER
(RC-20)

HERE LIES
THE REMAINS OF
ROBERT McCASLAN
WHO WAS BORN
MARCH 17th 1767
HE EMIGRATED TO AMERICA
FROM THE COUNTY
TYRONE, IRELAND
AND DEPARTED THIS LIFE
NOV. 27th 1849
AGED 82 YEARS 8 MONTHS
AND 10 DAYS
HE ACTED ON THE STAGE.

IN VIRTUOUS PATHS HE ALWAYS TROD
BUT NOW HE IS GONE TO DWELL WITH GOD.
(MC-7)

JANE VANDERHORST HEYWARD TRENHOLM BRADLEY
AUG 8, 1882 ------- APR. 14, 1957
GIFTED ARTIST AND NOTED DRAMATIST,
BUT FIRST OF ALL, A FAITHFUL
WIFE AND A DEVOTED MOTHER.
"SOMEHOW I FEEL NOT THE WEIGHT OF THE SOD,
IN MY HEART I AM SURE OF THE GOODNESS OF GOD."
J.V.H.T.B.
1956

(MC-5)

ELIZABETH MORRISON MIMS
FEB 25, 1862
JUNE 21, 1938
CHRISTIAN, ARTIST, LOVER OF THE
BEAUTIFUL AND GOD.
(EF-1)

IN MEMORY OF
*WILLIAM HENRY BROWN
SON OF
JOSHUA AND HARRIET BROWN
BORN MAY 22ND 1808
DIED SEPTEMBER 16TH 1883
AMERICAN PROFILIST
ARTIST
(CT-41)

*Brown was a master Profilist and Silhouettes artist (a serious art style during his lifetime). As his fame spread throughout 19th Century, much of his work was published and exhibited.

AUTHORS, PRINTERS & A PLOWMAN

1829 - 1867
HENRY TIMROD
POET
AND HIS ONLY CHILD
WILLIE
LIE BURIED HERE
1901
(RC-63)

*Poet and newspaperman, called the poet laureate of the Confederacy. Timrod's poem *Carolina* are the lyrics to the official State anthem and his work has influenced the music of Bob Dylan.

JOHN MILLER
PIONEER PRINTER AND PUBLISHER BORN IN
LONDON ENGLAND, DIED IN PENDLETON S.C.
1730 - 1809
AN ENGLISH GENTLEMAN

JOHN MILLER 2nd
LONDON, ENGLAND - PENDLETON, S.C.
1770 - 1826

JOHN MILLER 3rd
PENDLETON, S. C., BACHELORS RETREAT
1794 - 1876

TO THESE NOBLE MEN, THEIR WIVES AND THEIR
DESCENDENTS WHO REST IN THIS SACRED SOIL
IS THIS STONE LOVINGLY DEDICATED
(PK-5)

SACRED
TO THE MEMORY OF
A.S. WILLINGTON,
DIED FEBRUARY 2ND 1862
IN HIS 81ST YEAR
HE WAS SENIOR EDITOR OF
THE CHARLESTON COURIER
NEARLY SIXTY YEARS
"THE MEMORY OF
THE JUST IS BLESSED"
(CT-46)

*JAMES DICKEY
1923 - 1997
POET
FATHER OF
BRONWEN
KEVIN AND CHRISTOPHER
"I MOVE AT THE HEART OF THE WORLD"
(GT-1)

*Poet and novelist, known most for his novel *Deliverance*.

THOMAS JOHN ADAMS
BORN MARCH 12, 1847
DIED MAY 30, 1902

CONFEDERATE SOLDIER
EDITOR OF EDGEFIELD ADVERTISER
33 YEARS
(EF-7)

HERE LYES INTERR'D YE BODY
OF MR. ELEAZER PHILLIPS
JUN'R. HIS MAJESTY'S FIRST PRINTER
FOR YE PROVINCE OF SOUTH
CAROLINA. HE WAS BORN IN
BOSTON IN N. ENGL'ND & WAS YE
SON OF MR. ELEAZER & MRS.
LYDIA PHILLIPS NOW OF
CHARLESTOWN IN N. ENGL'ND. HE
DEPARTED THIS LIFE JULY 10TH
1732. AGED 21 YEARS & 10 MO.
(CT-52)

J. EDGAR POAC
(PLOWMAN)
1854 - 1936
"HE CUT THE EARTH
TO SUIT YOUR TASTE."
(CS-15)

THE MEDICAL PROFESSION

WILLIAM MAZYCK, MD
1875 – 1907
"HIS SUN WENT DOWN AT NOON"
BUT LEFT A BRILLIANT AFTERGLOW
OF PERSONAL PURITY,
FILIAL AFFECTION, AND UNTIRING
DEVOTION TO DUTY

ERECTED BY HIS FRIENDS OF
THE MEDICAL PROFESSION
AS A TOKEN OF THEIR ESTEEM
(CT-42)

IN THIS CHURCHYARD
IS BURIED
JOSIAH FLAGG
1763-1816

THE FIRST NATIVE BORN AMERICAN TO MAKE
DENTISTRY
HIS LIFE'S WORK.
AND THE FIRST TO CARRY TO ANY FOREIGN LAND
EVIDENCE OF AMERICAN DENTAL PROGRESS.
SOLDIER IN THE AMERICAN REVOLUTION
SAILOR IN THE WAR OF 1812
DIED IN CHARLESTON SEPTEMBER 16, 1816
ERECTED BY THE
SOUTH CAROLINA DENTAL ASSOCIATION
AND THE CITY OF CHARLESTON
1953
(CT-51)

ROBERT L. BRODIE, M.D.
DIED OCTOBER 2, 1913
ASS'T SURGEON U.S. ARMY,
1854 - 1861
SURGEON C.S. ARMY
1861 – 1865
"HE SAVED OTHERS,
HIMSELF, HE COULD NOT SAVE"
(CT-104)

TO THE MEMORY
OF
EDWARD HALL BARTON, M. D.
THE SON OF
SETH AND SARAH EMERSON
BARTON
WAS BORN IN BALTIMORE ON
THE 24th OF FEBRUARY 1795,
DIED AT COLUMBIA ON
THE 19th OF SEPTEMBER 1859.

GIFTED BY NATURE WITH A
FINE INTELLECT AND GUIDED
BY AN ARDENT LOVE OF SCIENCE
AND IMPELLED BY PHILANTHROPY
AND REGARDLESS OF EMOLUMENT,
HE BECAME A PUBLIC
BENEFACTOR BY DEVOTING
HIS MIND EXCLUSIVELY TO HIS
PROFESSION AND ENRICHING
THE MEDICAL LITERATURE OF
HIS DAY WITH THE RESULT
OF HIS RESEARCHES
(RC-4)

IN MEMORY
OF
THE HON'BLE
PETER FAYSSOUX, M.D.
WHO DIED IN 1795
AGED 50 YEARS
AND
MRS. ANN FAYSSOUX
HIS CONSORT
WHO DIED IN 1810
AGED 52 YEARS
SURGEON GENERAL
IN THE
AMERICAN REVOLUTION
FIRST PRESIDENT
MEDICAL SOCIETY
OF S.C.
STATES RIGHTS
STATESMAN
(CT-80)

IN
MEMORY OF
JOSEPH F. JOHNSON, M. D.
ENTERED INTO REST
AGED 58 YEARS, 5 MONTHS
AND 20 DAYS
LIFE'S CHECQUERED WARP THE MOTH
NO LONGER FRETS,
THE PULSELESS HEART IT'S WASTING
CARES FORGETS;
THE WIND STORM REST UPON
THE SUNLESS SHORE,
TIMES WAVES SHALL CHAFE THIS
BEATEN ROCK NO MORE
(BF-3)

P. W. CULLEN, MD.
WHO DIED OF YELLOW FEVER IN
SAVANNAH, GA.
ON THE 10th DAY OF OCTOBER A.D. 1854
AGED 30 YEARS

HE WAS A DUTIFUL SON,
AN AFFECTIONATE BROTHER, A KIND FRIEND
AND A SINCERE CHRISTIAN.
HE WAS A DISTINGUISHED AND SUCCESSFUL
IN HIS MEDICAL PROFESSION.
HE BATTLED WITH HEROIC FORTITUDE
IN BEHALF OF HIS FELLOW MAN
WITHOUT DISTINCTION, AGAINST PESTILENCE
WHICH LAID WASTE THE CITY OF SAVANNAH, AND
AFTER HIS BRETHREN HAD FALLEN
ALMOST TO A MAN BY HIS SIDE.
EXHAUSTED BY HIS LABORS
HE FELL A VICTIM ON THE THIRD ATTACK
OF THE PLAGUE
AND DIED AT THE POST OF DUTY AND HONOR
LAMENTED BY A GRATEFUL CITY.
R.I.P.
(RC-46)

TEACHERS & PREACHERS

PREACHING OVER BISHOP CAPERS

Beneath the pulpit of Washington Street United Methodist Church lies the body of the first Methodist Bishop to South Carolina....purely by coincidence!

The church was mistakenly torched by Sherman's raiders who mistook it for the First Baptist Church, the site of the First Confederate Convention. When it came time to rebuild the church, the original location was found to be an unsuitable site, and the new church was constructed over a portion of the cemetery.

By happenstance the pulpit was placed over the grave of Bishop Capers. His headstone now lays flat within the crawl space of the church.

WILLIAM TERTIUS CAPERS, D.D.
BORN JANUARY 20, 1825
CALLED HOME
SEPTEMBER 10, 1894

IN HIS MINISTRY, MERCY AND TRUST MET
TOGETHER, RIGHTEOUSNESS AND PEACE KISSED
EACH OTHER.
(RC-68)

REV. ATHALIA L. J. IRWIN
UNIVERSALIST MINISTER,
WIFE OF
G. W. IRWIN,
BORN SEPT. 23, 1862 ELDORADO, ARK.
DIED OCT. 6, 1915 COLTON CALIF.

OH, SEND ME OUT TO TELL
THE NATIONS OF A LOVE
THAT BARS NO SOUL OUTSIDE
THAT HEAVENLY HOME ABOVE.
A.L.J.I.
(RC-1)

ELLISON CAPERS,
BORN IN CHARLESTON OCTOBER 14th 1837,
DIED IN COLUMBIA APRIL 22nd 1908.

HE RENDERED UNTO CAESAR THE THINGS THAT ARE
CAESAR'S
AND UNTO GOD THE THINGS THAT ARE GOD'S.

ELLISON CAPERS.
BRIGADIER GENERAL
IN THE SOUTHERN CONFEDERACY.
SECRETARY OF STATE OF
SOUTH CAROLINA.
PRIEST OF THE
PROTESTANT EPISCOPAL CHURCH.
BISHOP OF THE
DIOCESE OF SOUTH CAROLINA.
CHANCELLOR OF THE
UNIVERSITY OF THE SOUTH
(RC-62)

THE REVD MR. JOHN LAMBERT
LATE MASTER PRECEPTOR & TEACHER OF GRAMMAR
AND OTHER ARTS & SCIENCES TAUGHT IN THE
FREE SCHOOL
AT CHARLES-TOWN FOR YE PROVINCE
OF SOUTH CAROLINA
AND AFTERNOON LECTURER OF THIS PARISH
OF SAINT PHILIP'S CHARLESTOWN
DEPARTED THIS LIFE (SUDDENLY)
ON YE 14TH OF AUG AD 1729
BLESSED IS THAT SERVANT WHOM HIS LORD WHEN
HE COMETH SHALL FIND SO DOING;
THEREFORE BE YE ALSO READY
(CT-40)

IN MEMORY OF
LIZZIE RICE
WIFE OF
REV. DR. J. W. WOLLING
BORN OCT. 24, 1852
DIED JULY 13, 1921
EIGHTEEN YEARS OF HER
LIFE SHE SPENT IN BRAZIL,
S. A. WITH DR. WOLLING IN
MISSION WORK.
(UN-4)

JENNIE L.
ALLEN
BORN JUNE 14, 1863
DIED MAY 23, 1963
"SHE TAUGHT LITTLE CHILDREN
TO COME UNTO HIM"
(AB-8)

IN MEMORY OF
COURTNEY SMITH KING, M.D.
BORN IN CHARLESTON, S.C. MAY 20, 1831,
AND DIED, AT KERTCH, RUSSIA
ON THE 19TH MARCH 1855
OF MALIGNANT TYPHUS FEVER
WHILE SERVING IN THE RUSSIAN IMPERIAL MEDICAL
STAFF DURING THE WAR
BETWEEN RUSSIA AND THE ALLIED POWERS
AGED23 YEARS, 9 MONTHS AND 27 DAYS
A DUTIFUL SON AND AFFECTIONATE BROTHER

NO BROTHER'S AND NO SISTER'S GENTLE TONE,
NO MOTHER'S TEAR
SOOTH'D THE LAST SIGH OF HIM WE MORN,
BUT GOD HIMSELF WAS THERE.
(CT-78)

IN MEMORY OF
REV. DAVID E. DUNLAP
AGED 56 YEARS & 5 MONTHS
ALSO OF
SUSANNA, HIS WIFE
AGED 30 YEARS & 8 MONTHS
THEY BOTH DIED ON THE
10th SEPTEMBER 1804

O'! DEATH, INSATIATE ARCHER
COULD NOT ONE SUFFICE?

REV. D. E. DUNLAP
WAS ORDAINED AND INSTALLED
FIRST PASTOR OF THIS CHURCH
JUNE 4, 1795.
(RC-37)

FIREMEN, POLICE, A JAILOR & SUPREME COURT JUSTICE

ERECTED
BY THE OFFICERS AND MEMBERS
OF THE VIGILANT FIRE ENGINE CO.
IN THE MEMORY OF
THEIR LATE VICE PRESIDENT
WILLIAM PRITGHARD
WHO DIED AUGUST 15TH, 1882
AGED 30 YEARS, 6 MONTHS
AND 4 DAYS
(CT-47)

MY BELOVED SON
JOHN HARLOW
BORN MAY 6, 1846
IN ROSCOMMON IRELAND
DIED DEC 22, 1878 FROM
WOUNDS RECEIVED ON
POLICE FORCE, WHILE IN
DISCHARGE OF HIS DUTY

THE ACTIONS OF THE BRAVE &
JUST, SMELL SWEET & BLOSSOM
IN THE DUST

ERECTED BY HIS
LOVING MOTHER
MAY HIS SOUL REST IN PEACE AMEN
(CT-100)

ERECTED
IN MEMORY OF
WILLIAM LENOX ESQr.
LATE
HIS BRITANNIA MAJESTY'S
COMMISSARY OF PRISONERS
WHO DIED
THE 16TH OF MAY 1781
AGED 29 YEARS

A BROTHER'S AFFECTION PAYS HIS LAST
TRIBUTE AT THE REMEMBRANCE OF A
LOVING RELATION; A STEADY FRIEND; A
GOOD MEMBER OF SOCIETY; AND A
SINCERE CHRISTIAN
(CT-79)

SACRED TO THE MEMORY OF
EUGENE BLACKBURN GARY
AUG 22, 1854 - DEC. 10, 1926
LIEUTENANT GOVERNOR
1890 - 1893
ASSOCIATE JUSTICE OF THE SUPREME COURT
1893 - 1912
CHIEF JUSTICE OF THE SUPREME COURT
1912 - 1926

"WELL DONE GOOD AND FAITHFUL SERVANT."
(AB-1)

BASEBALL, NASCAR & A POLITICAL ASSASSIN

*"BOBO"
LOUIS NORMAN NEWSOM
AUGUST 11, 1907
DECEMBER 7, 1962
(DG-1)

*Adorned with a glove, bat and ball, big league baseball player Bobo Newsom's epitaph is a short one considering he was a loquacious, but light-hearted braggart.

*BOB "HURRICANE" HAZLE
"WE LOVE YOU SO"
(RC-69)

*Hazel (1930–1992) was a major league baseball player with the Milwaukee Braves. At bat he had a .403 average he "blew away the ball" when he hit it earning him the nickname "Hurricane".

*R.A. "DICKIE" DIETZ
ALWAYS IN MY HEART
SEPT. 18, 1941
JUN 28, 2005
(GV-5)

*Dick (the Mule) Dietz was an outstanding major league pitcher. He was a big man with an equally big personality.

*JACKSON
JOSEPH W.
JULY 16, 1888
DEC. 5, 1951
(GV-1)

*This is the grave of baseball great "Shoeless" Joe Jackson who was implicated in the infamous Black Sox Scandal in 1919.

SMITH
NOAH L.
DEC. 27, 1906
MAR. 27, 1990

SMITH
AUTO PARTS

*LOUISE D.
JULY 31, 1916
APR. 15, 2006

FIRST LADY
OF NASCAR
(GV-4)

*Louise Smith (buried with her husband, owner of Smith Auto Parts) is the greatest female name in NASCAR. She was the first woman to be inducted into the Hall of Fame and the winner of 38 racing events.

THE POLITICAL ASSASSIN

"Lee" Atwater was Chairman of the RNC, advisor to Presidents Ronald Reagan and George H.W. Bush, political consultant and blues musician (Atwater played backup guitar for Percy Sledge and BB King). He was also a complex, intelligent individual and a master at political assassination. Most notable was the Willie Horton incident, where Atwater used a horrific crime committed during a prisoner's furlough to attack presidential hopeful Michael Dukakis, and it worked.

ATWATER
H. LEE
1951 - 1991
TEACHER, LEADER, HUSBAND.
FATHER, SON
I DO NOT CHOOSE TO BE A COMMON MAN
IT IS MY RIGHT TO BE UNCOMMON
I PREFER THE CHALLENGES
OF LIFE TO GUARANTEED SECURITY
THE THRILL OF FULFILLMENT TO THE
STATE CALM OF UTOPIA
I WILL NEVER COWER BEFORE ANY MASTER
SAVE MY GOD
REPUBLICAN CREED
(RC-70)

MARINERS & TRAIN ENGINEERS

TO THE MEMORY OF
JONAS GIRDLER
MARINER
A NATIVE OF MARBLEHEAD
WHO DEPARTED THIS LIFE THE 7TH
NOVEMBER 1803 AGED 28 YEARS.
THE BOREA'S BLAST AND NEPTUNE'S WAVES,
HAVE TOSSED ME TO AND FRO,
IN SPITE OF ALL BY GOD'S DECREE,
I HARBOUR HERE BELOW
WHILE I DO SAFE AT ANCHOR LIE,
WITH MANY OF OUR FLEET.
BUT I MUST ONCE AGAIN SET SAIL
MY SAVIOUR CHRIST TO MEET.

THIS STONE WAS ERECTED BY
JAMES M. POLLARD
(CT-67)

HERE LIES
THE BODY OF
CAPT WILLIAM ELLIOTT
MARINER
WHO DEPARTED THIS LIFE SEP 23RD 1790
AGED 40 YEARS 1 MONTH & 4 DAYS
IN HIM HE SAW THE SEAMAN PLAIN AND BOLD,
AN HONEST HEART AND FAITHFUL TO HIS TRUST,
NOW SAFE IN PORT HER VARIOUS VOYAGES DONE,
HIS BARQUE HAS DROPT HER ANCHOR IN THE DUST,
THOU WHO SHALT READ THE
NSCRIPTION ON THIS STONE,
MAKE ALL THE VIRTUES THAT WERE IN HIS YOUR
OWN.
(CT-68)

*ALLEN R. FRIPP
AUG 21, 1859
OCT 30, 1936
"A LOVER OF THE SEA"
"AT REST"
(CT-14)
*At the top of this headstone is a carving of a sailing ship.

WM. E. McCARTER
BORN COLUMBIA, S. C.
SEPT. 23, 1837
DIED BATH, S. C.
JULY 11, 1905
HE LAID HIS HAND ON THE
THROTTLE OF HIS ENGINE AND
RELEASED THE STEAM, WHEN
THE ANGEL OF DEATH BREATHED
ON HIS FACE; AND HE SLEPT.
(AK-6)

MY HUSBAND
W. L. WEATHERSBEE,
BORN
NOV. 29, 1868.
*KILLED BY THE FALLING
IN OF A TRESTLE ON
THE C. N. & L. R. R.
SEPT. 9, 1899.
BEYOND THE FAREWELL
AND THE PARTING, LOVE
REST AND HOME.
(RC-16)

*His death is graphically depicted on his headstone. Carved beneath his epitaph is a train running off the end of a trestle!

SLAVES, "MAMMIES" & INDIANS

IN MEMORY OF A GROUP OF
FAITHFUL SLAVES WHO ARE
BURIED HERE AND IN
TESTIMONY TO THE LOVE AND
RESPECT THAT EXISTED
BETWEEN MASTER AND SERVANT

THIS STONE WAS ERECTED BY
OLD PURITY SOCIETY
1942
(CS-11)

*DADDY TOM
A FAITHFUL AND HONEST SERVANT
DEPARTED THIS LIFE
THE 9TH DAY OF FEBRUARY 1857
BORN ON THIS PLACE BEFORE 1776
A KINDLY TEMPER, A CHEERFUL
OBEDIENCE AND WILLINGNESS TO WORK
CONCILIATED THE REGARD OF THUS
WHO TREATED HIM IN HIS
LIFE TIME, AS A FRIEND
AND CAUSED HIM WHEN HE DIED
TO BE BURIED LIKE A CHRISTIAN.
(MC-1)

*Daddy Tom's headstone was found just **outside** the walls
of the consecrated ground of the family cemetery.

TO THE MEMORY
OF THE
OLD
BLACK MAMMIES
OF THE
McFADDIN FAMILY

"GREEN BE THE TURF ABOVE THEE
FRIEND OF OUR BETTER DAYS
NONE KNEW THEE BUT TO LOVE THEE
NOR NAMED THEE BUT TO PRAISE"

"ON GREENER HILLS YOU SING TODAY
YORE CHILLUN HEAR THE ROUNDELAY"

"OUR SOUTHLAND IS BRIGHTER-BETTER
BECAUSE YOU PASSED THIS WAY"

ERECTED BY THE DESCENDENTS
OF THE
McFADDIN FAMILY
AND THE UNTIRING EFFORTS OF
DR. A. L. BLANDING
AND LOVINGLY DEDICATED
TO THEIR MEMORY

ERECTED 1941
(CD-1)

Front

1860
DEDICATED TO
THE FAITHFUL SLAVES
WHO, LOYAL TO A SACRED TRUST,
TOILED FOR THE SUPPORT
OF THE ARMY WITH MATCHLESS
DEVOTION AND STERLING
FIDELITY [AND] GUARDED OUR DEFENSELESS
HOMES, WOMEN AND CHILDREN DURING
THE STRUGGLE FOR THE PRINCIPLES
OF OUR "CONFEDERATE STATES OF
AMERICA."
1865

Back

1895
ERECTED BY SAM'L E. WHITE
IN GRATEFUL MEMORY OF EARLIER
DAYS. WITH APPROVAL OF THE
JEFFERSON DAVIS
MEMORIAL ASSOCIATION.
AMONG THE MANY FAITHFUL:
NELSON WHITE - ANTHONY WHITE
SANDY WHITE - JIM WHITE
WARREN WHITE - HENRY WHITE
SILAS WHITE - NATHAN SPRINGS
HANDY WHITE - SOLOMON SPRATT
(YK-1)

OCEOLA, FREEDOM FIGHTER

Oceola was of Creek Indian, and Scots-Irish decent. He was raised as a Creek and after their defeat by General Andrew Jackson in 1814, he assimilated into the Seminole nation. Soon becoming an influential Seminole warrior, he was instrumental in starting the Second Seminole War. Eventually captured, he was sent to Fort Marion in St. Augustine, Florida, later transferred to Fort Moultrie, SC where he became a folk hero of sorts.

OCEOLA
PATRIOT AND WARRIOR
DIED AT FORT MOULTRIE
JANUARY 30TH 1838
(CT-1)

OSENAPPA

The grave of Osenappa at the Old Stone Church Cemetery in Clemson, SC is alleged to be the only Native-American buried in a "white cemetery" during that 18th century. Nothing is known of his origins, or connections to the "white settlers who buried him. His grave is a traditional pile of stones (see Chapter 6 for a photograph of his grave).

1794
OSENAPPA
CHEROKEE INDIAN
(PK-4)

CHAPTER 8

WORDS OF WISDOM

"I will not be right back after this message"
.........................*Epitaph of Merv Griffin*

AGNES ELIZABETH
LARTIGUE
BORN JULY 13th 1855
DIED MAY 11th 1862
AGED 6 YEARS 9 MONTHS
& 11 DAYS
ONLY CHILD OF
GERALD R. & ULID LARTIGUE

FOUND PARENTS TEARING HER LOSS
SHE SOUGHT FROM EACH A KISS
AND GRIEVING FOR THEIR SORROW
SAID **"MA, KISS PA"**, AND THEN DIED
OF SUCH IS THE KINGDOM OF HEAVEN
(BW-3)

BENEATH
THIS MARBLE SLAB SLEEPS
THE REMAINS OF
A SINNER SAVED BY GRACE
SARAH MARGARET ZIMMERMAN
DAVIS
WIFE OF
WM. K. DAVIS
BORN SEPTEMBER 14th, 1815
DIED DECEMBER 29th, 1857
"I AM THE RESURRECTION OF THE LORD"

"THE INSCRIPTION UPON THIS TABLET
IS IN CONFORMITY TO THE WISHES OF
THE DECEASED."
(FF-3)

THOMAS GLASCOCK
BACON
BORN JUNE 24th,
1812,
DIED SEPTEMBER 25th,
1876.

COLONEL OF
7th REGIMENT, S. C. V.

**"LET ME GO! I WANT TO GO
TO MY REGIMENT...."**
HIS LAST WORDS.
(EF-4)

MY
HUSBAND
THOMAS R. BELL
WHOSE SUDDEN DEMISE WAS
CAUSED FROM DISEASE OF THE
HEART DECEMBER 23rd 1876
IN THE 52 YEAR OF HIS AGE

GOD LOOKED UPON THE LOVING,
NOBLE, GENEROUS HEART,
BATTLING WITH LIFE'S DISAPPOINTMENTS
& LOSSES UNTIL AT LAST,
LIKE GOLD REFINED, HIS BRUISED
SPIRIT LOOKED UP TO HIM
AND IN SUBMISSION HE CRIED,
"MY FATHER AND MY GOD!"
(FF-6)

J. A. DARRAGH
BORN
DEC. 10, 1857
DIED
MARCH 13, 1876.
HE DIED IN THE FULL HOPE OF
THE RESURRECTION.
HIS LAST WORDS WERE:
**"I AM GOING HOME TO MY MOTHER,
PA MEET ME IN HEAVEN"**
(AB-6)

CLARA ADELA
BELL
BORN FEBY. 23 rd 1859
DIED SEPT. 21st 1863
"AUNTIE, I DO LOVE JESUS!"
(FF-5)

DIED
MARCH 14th 1864
OF CAMP FEVER
AGED 17 YEARS AND 9 MONTHS
LIEUT. BENJAMIN TAYLOR
GIBBES
CO. D 16th REGT. S.C.V.
ARMY OF TENNESSEE
EIGHTH SON OF
DR. R. W. AND C. E. GIBBES
PURE IN HEART, CONFIDING IN HIS
SAVIOUR, HIS LAST WORDS WERE
"THANK GOD, I AM NOT AFRAID TO DIE."
(RC-59)

PAUL SARRATT
SON OF
S. M. & E. S. RICE
MARCH 18, 1891
OCT. 30, 1899

**"I AM GOING TO
HEAVEN RIGHT NOW
AND WILL SEE GOD."
(UN-1)**

JOHN C. MITCHELL
CAPTAIN,
1ST REGI. S.C. ARMY, C.S.A.
COMMANDING FORT SUMTER,
KILLED UPON THE PARAPET
DURING THE BOMBARDMENT,
JULY 20, 1864
AGED 26

**"I WILLINGLY GIVE MY LIFE FOR SOUTH CAROLINA;
OH! THAT I COULD HAVE DIED
FOR IRELAND!"**
HIS LAST WORDS

ERECTED BY HIS COMRADES
1878
(CT-95)

Front side:

ERECTED TO THE
MEMORY OF
ELIZABETH HUTCHINSON
JACKSON, MOTHER OF
ANDREW JACKSON
SEVENTH PRESIDENT
OF THE
UNITED STATES

Left side:

LAST WORDS TO HER SON:
**"MAKE FRIENDS
BY BEING HONEST,
KEEP THEM BY BEING'
STEADFAST. NEVER
TELL A LIE NOR TAKE
WHAT IS NOT YOUR OWN
NOR SUE FOR SLANDER."**

Right side:

IT WAS HER ZEAL FOR
ACCOMPLISHMENTS
THAT MADE HANDICAPS
SEEM TO RESOLVE
THEMSELVES IN HER
FAVOR WHICH ENABLED
THEM TO ENDURE THE
HARDSHIPS OF THE
GREAT WAGON ROAD
TO "THE GARDEN OF
THE WAXAWS!"
(LC-4)

CHAPTER 9

ASHES TO ASHES

"Good Friend for Jesus Sake Forbeare,
To Dig the Dust Enclosed Heare!
Blese be the Man that Spares these Stones,
And Curst be He that Moves My Bones."

Epitaph of William Shakespeare

THE THREE CREWS OF THE *H.L. HUNLEY*

During the Civil War the Union's naval blockade of Charleston, SC was so serious, that extreme measures were developed to "break the siege." The answer was a submarine designed and funded by Horace Lawson Hunley. Built in Mobile, Alabama by Hunley and Thomas W. Parks, the submarine was christened the *H.L. Hunley* and sent to Charleston.

On her first attempt to attack a Union ship on August 29, 1863, five of her eight-man crew died when an open hatch was flooded in error. Except for her commander, the crew was made up of civilian volunteers, unfamiliar with the submarine. The *Hunley* was raised and prepared to be used again.

Horace Hunley convinced the Confederacy bring in a crew from Mobile who were familiar with the ship. During a training mission on October 15, 1863 both Horace Hunley and Thomas Parks were on-board to supervise. The *Hunley* sank again, plunging to the bottom and killing all eight on board. Again, the submarine was raised and salvaged.

After months of repairs and testing, the *Hunley* was manned by a third volunteer crew who on February 17, 1864 attacked and sank the blockade ship, USS

Housatonic. Likely damaged by the blast, the *Hunley*, commanded by Lieutenant George Dixon, sank with her entire crew. When the *Hunley* was finally raised from the ocean floor in 2004, the remains of Dixon and his men were recovered and buried together at Magnolia Cemetery in Charleston. Nearby also lay the remains of Horace Hunley and Thomas Parks.

CAPT HORACE
L. HUNLEY
AGED 39 YEARS
OF LOUSIANA
A NATIVE OF TENNESSEE
HE LOST HIS LIFE IN THE
SERVICE OF HIS COUNTRY
ON THE 15TH OF OCT. 1863
(CT-106)

IN MEMORY
OF
THOMAS W. PARKS
WHO LOST HIS LIFE IN THE
DEFENSE OF CHARLESTON HARBOR
OCTOBER 15TH 1863
AGED 33 YEARS
HE DOUTH ALL THINGS WELL
(CT-107)

LIEUT
GEORGE E. DIXON
H.L. HUNLEY
CSA
FEB 17, 1864
(CT-108)

THE LONG CAIN MASSACRE

Before the American Revolution one of the boundaries of the Cherokee Nation was marked by the Long Cain Creek. By 1760, because of rising tensions, about 150 white settlers in the area banded together to relocate to Augusta, Georgia. As they made their way south they were attacked by Cherokee warriors, who killed and scalped 23 including women and children.

PATR. CALHOUN SR.
IN MEMORY OF MRS.
CATHERINE CALHOUN
AGED 76 YEARS WHO
WITH 22 OTHERS WAS
HERE MURDERED BY
THE INDIANS THE
FIRST OF FEB. 1760
(MC-11)

IN MEMORY OF
MARY WINIFRED PATRICK
NORRIS
ELIZA WRENTZ NORRIS
EZEKIEL NORRIS
WILLIAM NORRIS
SARAH NORRIS
DIED HERE
1 FEBRUARY 1760
LONG CANE MASSACRE
ERECTED BY THE
DESCENDENTS OF
ROBERT NORRIS
(MC-12)

CHARLESTON, A NICE PLACE TO LIVE....
....BUT NOT TO VISIT

IN MEMORY
OF JAMES RICHARDSON
A NATIVE OF WESTMORELAND ENGLAND
FOR MANY YEARS A RESIDENT
MERCHANT IN HAVANA
WHILST ON A VISIT TO THIS CITY
FOR THE BENEFIT OF HIS HEALTH,
HE DEPARTED THIS LIFE
ON THE 13TH OF MARCH 1831
AGED 41 YEARS
(CT-22)

SACRED TO THE MEMORY OF
MR. ANDREW BRADSHAW OF BOSTON
WHO WAS BORN AT MEDFORD MASS.
23RD JULY 1793
AND DIED 17TH MARCH 1829
IN THE 36TH YEAR OF HIS AGE
WHILE ON A VISIT TO THIS CITY FOR
THE BENEFIT OF HIS HEALTH
(CT-53)

SACRED
TO THE MEMORY OF
MR. HENRY TUTHILL,
A NATIVE OF NEW YORK.
WHO DIED JAN. 10TH 1819,
WHILE HERE ON A VISIT FOR THE
BENEFIT OF HIS HEALTH.
MODEST AND UNASSUMING IN HIS DEPORTMENT,
FAITHFUL AND HONEST IN HIS DEALINGS, HE
LIVED RESPECTED, AND DIED LAMENTED.
(CT-66)

IN MEMORY
R. HAUSMANN,
& F. POTMANN,
MURDERED NOV. 1876
NEAR AIKIN
FAR FROM THEIR NATIVE LAND,
THEY SLEEP THEIR DREAMLESS SLEEP,
A SLUMBER CALM AND DEEP,
A SILENT MIDNIGHT IN THE TOMB
(AK-4)

MAN. V 1822
MR. ARGENEE
A FRENCH TUTOR IN THE MORRIS FAMILY
AND WHO, WITH THEM,
WAS KILLED IN THE HURRICANE OF 1822
AND SAID TO HAVE BEEN PLACED
IN THE MANIGAULT VAULT
THERE IS NO RECORD TO CONFIRM THIS
(CT-48)

IN MEMORY OF JAMES EDMUND
A NATIVE OF
GLASGOW, SCOTLAND
AND A RESIDENT OF
CAMDEN, S. C. WHO DIED
AT McCORD'S FERRY IN
OCTOBER 1820,
AGED 35 YEARS,
OF FEVER CONTRACTED WHILE
DREDGING THE WATEREE
RIVER.
(KS-16)

YESTERDAY FOR ME
& TODAY FOR THEE
HERE LIES THE BODY OF
MR. THOMAS POOL WHO WAS BORN AT GOSPORT
THE 20TH APRIL 1717
AND WAS UNFORTUNATELY CASTAWAY
ON THE BAR OF THIS HARBOUR ON THE
20TH MARCH 1754. AGED 37 YEARS.
HE WAS A SOBER INDUSTRIOUS AND SKILFUL PILOT,
OBLIGING IN HIS CONVERSATION, A KIND
HUSBAND, A TENDER PARENT AND A USEFUL
MEMBER OF SOCIETY & WAS MUCH REGRETTED BY
EVERY ONE THAT KNEW HIM
(CT-38)

SACRED
TO THE MEMORY OF
ANGUS McKAY,
SON OF
J. J. AND S. E. BRABHAM.
WHO WAS BORN MAY 20th 1852.
AND KILLED BY THE FALLING OF THE
MASONIC LODGE AT BAMBERG, S. C.
JUNE 5th 1866
AGED 15 YEARS AND 15 DAYS

"PRIDE OF OUR HEARTS, FAREWELL AWHILE,
OUR EARTHLY COURSE WILL SOON BE O'VER,
WE SOON SHALL GREET THY PARTING SMILE
AND MEET TO PART NO MORE"
(BB-4)

*IN MEMORY
OF W. G. HAZEL, M. D.
1828   1893
DROWNED IN THE STORM
OF AUG. 27th

"HIDE ME, O MY SAVIOR, HIDE,
TILL THE STORM OF LIFE BE PAST;
SAFE INTO THE HAVEN GUIDE,
O, RECEIVE MY SOUL AT LAST"
(BF-8)

*One of over 2,000 victims of the Great Sea Islands
Hurricane and Tidal Wave of 1893, the second deadliest in
US History.

SACRED
TO
THE MEMORY
OF
JOS. K. ALEXANDER
WHO WAS BORN 8th MAY, 1838
AND CAME TO HIS DEATH
BY THE ACCIDENTAL DISCHARGE
OF HIS GUN
WHILE ENGAGED IN SPORTING
ON SATURDAY
THE 4th OF FEB. 1854
THIS STONE IS ERECTED
BY HIS SORROWING SCHOOLMATES
AS A TRIBUTE TO HIS STERLING WORTH
HE WAS A MEMBER OF THE
METHODIST EPISCOPAL CHURCH
AND AMONG HIS LAST WORDS WERE;
"JESUS IS PRECIOUS TO MY SOUL."
(KS-8)

*SACRED
TO THE MEMORY OF
WILLIAM C. LeGRAND
AGED 18 YEARS
WHO WAS DROWNED ON THE
MEMORABLE 5th MAY, 1860 AT
BOYKINS POND

*SACRED
TO THE MEMORY OF
MY HUSBAND
LUCIUS H. LeGRAND
AGED 31 YEARS
WHO WAS DROWNED ON THE
MEMORABLE 5th MAY, 1860 AT
BOYKINS POND
(KS-5)

*These two stones of father and son were found side by side.

IN
MEMORY OF
FRAZEE
BRITTIN
WHO WAS CRUSHED
UNDER FALLING
WALLS AT A FIRE
DEC. 14th 1868
AGED 19 YEARS OLD
SON OF
A.B.mC. & EMELINE
SQUIRE
(RC-36)

156

IN MEMORY OF
ISABELLA BOYLE
OF
GLASGOW, SCOTLAND,
WHO RETURNED FEVER
STRICKEN FROM THE DEATH
BED OF HER HUSBAND
JAMES EDMUND
AND DIED IN CAMDEN, S. C.
IN OCTOBER 1820,
LEAVING THREE HELPLESS
ORPHANS HERE AND ONE
BEYOND THE SEA
(KS-9)

GEORGE AUGUSTUS CLOUGH
A NATIVE OF LIVERPOOL
DIED SUDDENLY OF STRANGER'S DISEASE
NOVR. 5TH 1843
AGED 22
(CT-21)

IN MEMORY OF
EDWARD WATIES WARING
BORN JANUARY 14, 1921
LOST IN THE WATERS OFF
SULLIVAN'S ISLAND
JULY 27, 1928
(CT-105)

THIS MARBLE
IS ERECTED BY JAMES McKENZIE
IN MEMORY OF HIS LAMENTED BROTHER
M. WILLIAM McKENZIE
A NATIVE OF NISBER MILL ROXBURGHSHIRE
SCOTLAND
WHO HAVING COMPLETED THE ARDUOUS TASK OF
CONSTRUCTING A DAM ACROSS BROAD RIVER
NEAR THE MOUTH OF SALUDA
WAS UNFORTUNATELY DROWNED
ON THE 26th OF JULY, 1823
ON THE VERY SPOT OF HIS INDEFATIGABLE ACTION
IN THE 11th YEAR OF HIS AGE.
(RC-23)

SACRED
TO THE MEMORY OF
GENERAL WILLIAM A. BULL
WHO WAS AN ELEGANT AND POLITE SCHOLAR, A
GENTLEMAN,
A WARM ZEALOUS AND DISTINGUISHED PATRIOT
A BRAVE AND MOST GENEROUS OFFICER AND WAS
THUS
ENDEARED TO ALL RANKS OF MEN WHO KNEW HIM.
A KIND NEIGHBOR, A VERY WARM AND DEVOTED
FRIEND,
KIND AND LIBERAL TO THE POOR, A GOOD
AND GENEROUS BROTHER.

INCREDIBLE TO RELATE! ON THE NIGHT OF
THE 27TH OF DEC. 1838, BEING ALONE ON HIS
PLANTATION,
GENERAL BULL WAS MOST UNJUSTLY, CRUELLY AND
HORRIBLY MURDERED BY HIS OWN SERVANTS !
AGED 49 YEARS AND 4 MONTHS
MC-4

SACRED
TO THE MEMORY OF
THOMAS F. PORCHER
OF WHITEHALL
ONLY SON OF
THOMAS AND CATHERINE PORCHER
AGED 33 YEARS
DROWNED
IN THE SURF OF SULLIVAN'S ISLAND
AUGUST 17TH 1861
IN THE ATTEMPT TO RESCUE HIS SISTER
AND NIECE
THE EARTH AND THE SEA SHALL
GIVE UP THEIR DEAD
(CT-86)

IN MEMORY OF
*F. WELLS
WHO DEPARTED THIS LIFE NOVR. 18TH 1794
AGED 11 YEARS, I MONTH AND 18 DAYS

AH! HAPLESS FRANCES, LET THE FRIENDLY MUSE,
TO THY STONE TOMB THE TRAGIC TALE IMPART
NOR LET THY SHADE THE FRIENDLY BOON REFUSE
'TIS THE LAST TRIBUTE OF A FRIENDLY HEART.

WHAT! THO' A VICTIM TO THE WRATHLESS FLAMES;
THY RISING CHARMS UNTIMELY DID EXPIRE:
'TIS HEAVEN, WHO ONLY SUCH PERFECTION CLAIMS,
CONSUMED TO KINDLE SERAPHIC FIRE.
(CT-30)
The victim of a fire.

ALSO TO THE MEMORY
OF MRS. THEODOSIA ROSS,
HER DAUGHTER MRS. ANN GREGORIE,
AND ANN ELIZABETH THEODOSIUS
CHILDREN OF
JAMES AND ANN GREGORIE
WHO PERISHED AT SEA IN THE SHIP EARL OF
GALLOWAY
ON THEIR PASSAGE FROM LONDON TO THIS PLACE
IN THE YEAR 1784
LONG PARTED FRIENDS IN HEAVEN MEET
TO PART NO MORE.
(CT-81)

SACRED TO THE MEMORY
OF
WILLIAM GEORGE BROWN
ONLY CHILD OF
WILLIAM & MAGDALEN BROWN
WHO DEPARTED THIS LIFE BY FALLING IN
BETWEEN CRAFTS WHARF & THE SIP
UNITED STATES & WAS DROWNED NOV THE 29
1811 AGED 14 YEARS & ELEVEN DAYS
HIS BODY RESTORED TO HIS DISTRESSED
PARENTS THE NEXT DAY & BY THEM
DEPOSITED BENEATH THIS HUMBLE STONE
HIS DESERVING VIRTUES & TALENTS GAVE
A HAPPY PRESAGE TO HIS FOND PARENTS OF
HIS FUTURE USEFULNESS & COMFORT
BUT HEAVEN FOR WISE PURPOSES UNSEEN
SAW FIT TO DROP THIS FAIR FLOWER IN THE BUD
ERE IT HAD LOST IT'S HEAVENLY FRAGRANCE
& LOST HIS DISCONSOLATE PARENTS
TO MORN HIS EARLY DEATH
(CT-34)

WILLIAM SPENCER BROWN
BORN IN BROWNVILLE
NEW YORK
MAY 28th 1815,
WAS DROWNED IN ATTEMPTING
TO DESCEND BROAD RIVER
DURING THE *FRESHET.
AUGUST 30th 1852
(RC-61)

*A Flash Flood

J.C.E. RICHARDSON
BORN AUG 3RD 1826
DIED SEPT 14TH 1886
FROM INJURIES RECEIVED
DURING THE EARTHQUAKE*
AUGUST 1ST
(CT-96)

*The Charleston Earthquake of 1886 was one of the most powerful and damaging to ever affect the eastern United States. About one hundred people were killed, over two thousand buildings damaged with a cost of about six million dollars (over one hundred and fifty million dollars in today's economy).

MARY (POLLY) AUSTON
DAUGHTER OF
NATHANIEL AND AGNES
AUSTIN
KILLED BY INDIANS IN
THE INDIAN WAR THAT
PRECEDED THE REVOLUTION
(GV-7)

161

IN LOVING MEMORY
OF MY SISTER
ELIZA ANNE PHILLIPS
WHOSE REMAINS MINGLE HERE WITH
THE ASHES OF HER GREAT GRAND AUNT
IN THE HOPE OF JOYFUL
RESURRECTION
BORN AUG 22, 1822
DIED NOV 9, 1875
THEY THAT SOW IN TEARS
ALL REAP JOY
(CT-55)

MODEST
AND UNASSUMING AS THIS PALE MARBLE WAS,
THE YOUTH
WHOSE REMAINS ARE INTOMBED BENEATH ITS SHADE
THOMAS WARINGTON
BORN IN LONDON
FOUND A GRAVE IN CHARLESTON
IN THE OPENING BLOOM OF HIS 17TH YEAR ON THE
9TH DAY OF AUGUST 1796
HE FELL VICTIM TO A MALIGNANT FEVER
THEN RAGING IN THIS CITY
IN HIM DIED THE EARLY PROMISE OF
AN ORNAMENT TO SOCIETY
AND THE PROP OF THAT
FATHER'S AGE
WHO DEDICATES THIS HUMBLE STONE
TO THE MEMORY
OF A GOOD AND MOST
BELOVED SON.
(CT-23)

SACRED
TO THE MEMORY OF
BENJAMIN JENKINS GRIMBALL
WHO DEPARTED THIS LIFE
AFTER A PAINFUL ILLNESS
OF FIVE MONTHS
MORE THAN THREE OF WHICH
HE SUFFERED WHILE AT SCHOOL
IN PHILADELPHIA
HE WAS MILD
AND AMIABLE IN HIS MANNERS.
AFFECTIONATE IN HIS DISPOSITION;
AND AS HIS DISEASE PROGRESSED,
HE BECAME PERFECTLY RESIGNED
TO HIS FATE;
EXPRESSING ONLY AN ANXIOUS DESIRE
TO DIE AT HOME
BORN 3RD MAY 1820
DIED 27TH JULY 1838
IN THE 19TH YEAR OF HIS AGE
(CT-9)

IN MEMORY OF
OTIS
SECOND SON OF OTIS J. AND MARY A CHAFEE
WHO DROWNED WHILE BATHING
IN THE SWANNANOA RIVER
NEAR ASHEVILLE, NO. CA.
ON THE 1rst OF AUGUST 1857
AGED 13 YEARS AND 21 DAYS
"FATHER NOT OUR WILL BUT
THINE BE DONE"
(CT-45)

FATAL
ACCIDENT
IN THE MIDST OF LIFE WE ARE IN
DEATH!
13 YRS, 1MO AND 19 DAYS,
TERMINATED THE EXISTENCE OF MASTER
CHARLES CLEARY

HAPLESS BOY! ON THE 31ST OF MAY 1813,
ACCIDENTALLY FELL FROM THE LOFTY WALLS
OF ST PAUL'S CHURCH, WHEN THE IMMORTAL
PART INSTANTLY ASCENDED TO THE CHURCH
TRIUMPHANT ON HIGH, THE ABODE OF
UNIMBODIED SPIRITS, FROM WHOSE
BOURNE NO TRAVELER RETURNS.
BEREAVED PARENTS, BROTHERS AND SISTERS,
ALSO, YE YOUTHFUL COMPANIONS, COME
HITHER, BEHOLD THE NARROW LODGING.
READ, GO AWAY, REFLECT, RETURN AGAIN,
AND VIEW THE EARLY FATE OF YOUR BELOVED
CHARLES.
(CT-62)

COL. ARCHIBALD
KENNEDY
PATTON
BORN
MAY 24, 1819
FELL AT SHILOH
APR. 6, 1862
AND WAS BURIED ON
THE BATTLE FIELD
(MC-6)

ERECTED BY
MANY CITIZENS
OF ST. PETER'S PARISH
TO THE MEMORY OF
ROBERT E. SWEAT
OF WASHINGTON,
LIGHT INFANTRY,
HAMPTON'S LEGION
So. Ca. VOLUNTEERS
WHO DIED AT
CULPEPPER C. H. Va.
ON 19th AUGUST 1861
OF A WOUND IN THE
LEFT ARM RECEIVED
AT MANASSAS PLAINS
ON THE MEMORABLE
21rst JULY '61
AGED 24 YEARS, 6 MOS.
AND 26 DAYS.
(AL-1)

IN MEMORY
OF
JOHN HUNTER
SECOND OFFICER
BRITISH STEAMSHIP, BEDFORD
KILLED DURING THE GREAT
COTTON FIRE AT CHARLESTON
OCT. 17, 1880
AGED 34 YEARS

THIS STONE IS ERECTED
BY A FEW FRIENDS
(CT-90)

WIFE & DAUGHTER
LOST ON
S.S. CHAMPION
OFF
DELAWARE CAPES
NOV. 7, 1879

THEY WERE LOVELY
AND PLEASANT IN
THEIR LIVES,
AND IN THEIR DEATH
THEY WERE NOT DIVIDED.
(CT-89)

"I AM THE RESURRECTION AND THE LIFE"
ANN PORTER
DIED JULY 20, 1845
AGED 32 YEARS
ELIZA PORTER
DIED NOV. 29, 1849
AGED 22 YEARS
NATIVES OF BUNDON, IRELAND

BENEATH THIS TOMB REPOSE THE MORTAL REMAINS
OF
THESE GOOD SISTERS,
WHO UNITED BY BONDS OF LOVE THRO LIFE
ENJOY THE PRIVILEGE OF HAVING THEIR EARTHLY
PARTS
COMMINGLED AFTER DEATH.
MAY THEY REST IN PEACE, AMEN.
(AK-3)

*SAMUEL P. BAILEY
AGED 59

\-

AND ON HER
GRAND FATHER'S BOSOM
SLEEPETH
LITTLE MARY
THE FIRST BORN OF
S. H. & L. E. BAILEY
AGED 4.
(RC-5)

A Grandfather and Granddaughter buried together.

SACRED
TO THE
MEMORY OF
MARTHA C. McILIVANE
WIFE OF ROLF S. McILIVANE
AND DAUGHTER OF
J&J MONTGOMERY
WHO DIED OCTOBER 16TH 1824
IN THE 22ND YEAR OF
HER AGE

\-

*"AS SOON AS A MOTHER A CORPSE"
(LC-2)

She died during childbirth.

IN MEMORIAM
*ARTHUR BELIN FLAGG, M.D.
SEPT. 1, 1828
GEORGIANA WARD FLAGG
AUG. 8, 1833

"IN MEMORY OF MY LOVING FATHER AND MOTHER
WHO WERE SWEPT AWAY BY THE TIDAL WAVE ON
MAGNOLIA BEACH OCT. 13, 1893"
(GT-3)

*One of the brothers of Alice the Ghost of the Hermitage.
Eight of the Flagg and/Ward families perished during this
deadly hurricane.

IN MEMORY
OF
*ARTHUR ALFRED GILLING
A NATIVE OF LONDON ENGLAND,
BORN 19TH OF JUNE, 1811
AND DIED 12TH FEB., 1839

PREPARE TO MEET THY GOD!
(CT-3)

*According to church records, Gilling died as the result of a
dual on "the Sands", a level stretch of ground at Edingsville
Beach, Edisto Island. Strangely, the man who killed him
paid for and placed the inscription on his headstone.

SACRED
TO THE MEMORY OF
MRS. MARY ANN KILLIAN
CONSORT OF ELI KILLIAN
WHO DEPARTED THIS LIFE
JULY 31st 1844
AFTER AN ILLNESS OF EIGHT
DAYS AND GIVING BIRTH TO A
FEMALE INFANT
THEY BOTH REPOSE IN THIS
COMMON GRAVE
AGED 23 YEARS
10 MONTHS.
(RC-25)

IN MEMORIAM
B. F. RANDOLPH,
LATE SENATOR
FOR ORANGEBURG COUNTY
AND CHAIRMAN REPUBLICAN
STATE CENTRAL COMMITTEE
WHO DIED AT HODGES STATION
ABBEVILLE COUNTY
AT THE HANDS OF ASSASSINS
ON FRIDAY, OCT. 16,
A.D. 1868.
(RC-79)

TO THE MEMORY OF
*COL. PATRICK FERGUSON
SEVENTY-FIRST REGIMENT
HIGHLAND LIGHT INFANTRY
BORN IN ABERDEENSHIRE
SCOTLAND IN 1744
KILLED OCTOBER 7, 1780
IN ACTION AT
KING'S MOUNTAIN
WHILE IN THE COMMAND OF
THE BRITISH TROOPS

A SOLDIER OF MILITARY
DISTINCTION AND OF HONOR

THIS MEMORIAL
IS FROM THE CITIZENS OF
THE UNITED STATES OF AMERICA
IN TOKEN OF THEIR APPRECIATION
OF THE BONDS OF FRIENDSHIP AND
PEACE BETWEEN THEM AND THE
CITIZENS OF THE BRITISH EMPIRE

ERECTED OCTOBER 7, 1930
(YK-1)

After his death Ferguson was buried near the battle ground using the traditional Scottish method of piling stones upon the grave called a "cairn". The cairn still exists today.

CHAPTER 10

CAROLINA, CAROLINA!

"Hold up the Glories of thy Dead;
Say How thy Elder Children Bled,
and Point to Eutaw's Battle-Bed,
Carolina!"

Taken from the poem "CAROLINA" by Henry Timrod

FROM WEALTH TO SOLDIER TO POLITICS

Daniel de Saussure, before the Revolution, was one of the most successful merchants in Charleston, South Carolina which was also one of the wealthiest cities in Colonial America.

All of that changed with the Siege of Charleston by the British in 1780. During the seige, de Saussure fought along side his sixteen year old son, Henry William de Saussure, and both were captured by the overwhelming forces of the British Army. His son was sent to a prison ship in Charleston Harbor and the elder de Saussure was sent to prison in St. Augustine. His substantial properties seized by the British, and his remaining family exiled to Philadelphia.

After the war, he returned to Charleston and rebuilt much of his former wealth and established his family as one of most influential in Charleston politics and business.

SACRED
TO THE MEMORY OF
*DANIEL de SAUSSURE, ESQ.
A NATIVE OF THIS STATE,
WHO DEPARTED THIS LIFE, DEEPLY LAMENTED,
ON THE 2ND OF JULY 1798, AE 63 YEARS & 2 MONTHS
IN THE OCCUPATIONS OF COMMERCE,
WHICH FOR 42 YEARS HE STEADILY PURSUED,
HE WAS RESPECTED EQUALLY FOR HIS TALENTS,
INDUSTRY, AND INTEGRITY

HIS PATRIOTISM
EARLY EMBARKED HIM IN THAT REVOLUTION,
WHICH GAVE INDEPENDENCE TO HIS COUNTRY.
RESOLUTELY ENCOUNTERING THE FATIGUES OF
SERVICE,
PATIENTLY SUBMITTING TO THE LOSS OF PROPERTY,
AND FIRMLY SUSTAINING, WITH A BAND OF HIS
COMPATRIOTS,
A PAINFUL EXILE TO ST. AUGUSTINE.

IN THE LEGISLATURE, AND AS PRESIDENT OF THE
SENATE,
HE WAS HONORED WITH THE PUBLIC CONFIDENCE.

AS A HUSBAND AND FATHER ,
HE WAS DISTINGUISHED FOR HIS TENDERNESS AND
AFFECTION,
AND UNITED A LARGE CIRCLE OF CONNECTIONS
IN THE BOUNDS OF HARMONY AND LOVE.

AS A CITIZEN REVERED, VALUED AS A FRIEND,
AND FOR EQUANIMITY AND BENEVOLENCE NO LESS
ESTEEMED.
HE SUNK INTO THE TOMB FULL OF YEARS AND HONOR,
WITH A MIND PLACID, FROM LIFE WELL SPENT,
AND A LIVELY FAITH IN HIS BLESSED REDEEMER.
"WISDOM IS THE GREY HAIRS OF A MAN."
"AND AN UNSPOTTED LIFE IS OLD AGE."
(CT-73)

THE ORIGINAL G-MAN

FBI Special agent Melvin Purvis was the original "G-Man". He led the group that went after and gunned down John Dillinger (1933), and Pretty Boy Floyd (1934). He was such a popular figure at the time that FBI Director J. Edgar Hoover became so jealous he drove Purvis out of the agency. Never one to forget, Hoover continued to make Purvis' professional and private life difficult and he faded into obscurity. In 1960 Purvis shot himself in the head in an apparent suicide.

PURVIS

*"SAEPE TIMUI SED
NUMQUAM CUCURRI"

MELVIN HORACE PURVIS, JR
SON OF JANE ELIZABETH
AND MELVIN HORACE PURVIS, SR.
BORN OCTOBER 24, 1908
DIED FEBRUARY 29, 1960
MARRIED MARIE ROSANNE WILCOX
SEPTEMBER 4, 1933
CHILDREN MELVIN HORACE
PHILIP ALSTON WILCOX
CHRISTOPHER PERONNEAU
(FL-1)

*"I was Often Afraid,
But I Never Ran"

THE WAKE OF ANDREW JACKSON, SR.

The traditional story told in the Waxaw community relates that soon after the senior Jackson had passed away in his deathbed during a cold night in February, his coffin was placed on a sled and dragged from farmhouse to farmhouse in the style of the traditional Irish wake.

The wake turned into a two day movable party and much whiskey was consumed. By the time they had decided to bury Jackson and make their way to the cemetery of the Waxaw Church, the intoxicated mourners realized Jackson's coffin was not on the sled. The Waxaws quickly sobered up, especially given that their community had a history of religious worship filled with tinges of witchcraft and a strong belief in black magic.

Retracing their path to a place called Sugar Creek, they found that Jackson's casket had been raked off the sled by a low hanging branch. The lid had opened and Jackson's corpse was sitting up, waiting for them. When they finally made it back to the Church, it was dark and Jackson was buried under the light of smoking torches.

HERE LIES BURIED
ANDREW JACKSON, SR.
FATHER OF THE 7TH PRESIDENT
OF THE UNITED STATES
BORN IN IRELAND
DIED FEBRUARY 1767
(LC-3)

THE GHOST OF ALICE

ALICE
(GT-2)

This simple epitaph on a marble slab marks the grave of Alice Flagg (1834 – 1849), a member of a well-to-do low-country family. Alice and her widowed mother were invited by Alice's brother, Dr. Allard Flagg, to move into his new home, the Hermitage in Murrells Inlet.

The family easily entered into the high society of wealthy planters, enjoying their company while attending fine dinners and balls given by the wealthy plantation owners. Despite this Alice soon fell in love with a lumberman, who was "below her station". Her brother and guardian forbade Alice from seeing him. Unknown to her brother, the two were secretly engaged before she left for school, and she wore his ring on a ribbon around her neck.

While at school in Charleston, she contracted malaria and was sent home, only to die just upon arriving at the Hermitage. After her death her brother discovered the ring and angrily flung it into the nearby marsh. Alice is said to haunt the building and grounds of the Hermitage, looking for her lost ring.

THE FATHER OF SECESSION

He was born Robert Barnwell Smith, but he changed his last name to Rhett, after a well-known colonial relative, most famous for capturing Stede Bonnet (the gentleman pirate). Reinventing himself, Rhett entered public life, as a secessionist politician, racist, and owner of the Charleston Mercury, a pro State's Rights newspaper.

Sometimes called the "father of secession", Rhett along with John C. Calhoun, set the groundwork for the intellectual and political arguments supporting States Rights.

R. BARNWELL RHETT
DECEMBER 21, 1800
SEPTEMBER 14, 1876
ATTORNEY GENERAL S.C. 1832
MEMBER OF CONGRESS 1837-1847
UNITED STATES SENATOR 1850-1852
MEMBER OF CONFEDERATE PROVISIONAL
CONGRESS 1861
LEADING DEFENDER OF STATES RIGHTS
PARAMOUNT ADVOCATE OF SECESSION
(CT-83)

THE BURIAL, REBURIAL AND REBURIAL
OF JOHN C. CALHOUN

Along with Andrew Jackson & Strom Thurmond, John C. Calhoun was one of the three most influential statesmen South Carolina ever produced. A true genius, a master orator, a political pragmatist and one of the most politically powerful men of his day. However, he was also pro-slavery and the driving force behind the Southern "States Rights" movement. When he died, he was buried with honors in a special place near Charleston's magnificent St. Phillips Episcopal Church.

According to local stories when Charleston was under siege by Union forces, it was feared the "invaders" might desecrate Calhoun's Grave, which was located across the street from St. Phillips, in their non-church side of the cemetery. Calhoun's body & casket was exhumed and moved to lie next to his wife, a native of Charleston, who was buried in her family's plot adjacent to the church.

Sometime after the war, it was remembered that his body had been moved. The problem was the church-side of the cemetery was reserved only for long-standing church members and natives of Charleston. A debate was waged and in the end, Calhoun's casket was moved back across the street to his original burial spot in the non-church side cemetery.

JOHN CALDWELL CALHOUN

BORN MARCH 18, 1782;
DIED MARCH 31, 1850

REPRESENTATIVE
IN THE LEGISLATURE;
MEMBER OF CONGRESS

SECRETARY
OF WAR;
VICE PRESIDENT;
SECRETARY OF STATE

UNITED STATES
SENATOR

ERECTED
BY THE STATE OF
SOUTH CAROLINA
(CT-39)

DOCTOR COOPER'S HEADSTONE

Dr. Thomas Cooper was the 2nd President of South Carolina College (the future University of South Carolina for which the library is named for him). He was a friend of Thomas Jefferson who once called him, "one of the ablest men in America". Cooper was a Deist, a confirmed bachelor, and he shared similar beliefs on religion and politics as Jefferson. Cooper's views put him far ahead of his contemporaries and he was a critic of the Presbyterian leanings of those who controlled the college. He eventually resigned from the college in 1833 amid controversy and personal attacks.

Since Cooper had no religious affiliation when he died in 1839, the question arose, "where should the great man be buried?" The Guignard family agreed to allow his burial in their plot at Trinity Cathedral across the street from the State Capitol and a fitting monument for his grave was commissioned and inscribed, "Erected by his fellow citizens."

At once, great outrage ensued by Cooper's enemies and those who found his religious and political views offensive and very quickly his headstone was revised to read, "Erected by **a portion** of his fellow citizens."

ERECTED,
BY A PORTION OF
HIS FELLOW
CITIZENS,
TO THE MEMORY
OF
THOMAS COOPER,
M.D. & L.L.D.
FORMER PRESIDENT
OF
THE SOUTH
CAROLINA COLLEGE
BORN IN ENGLAND
DIED
AT COLUMBIA,
MAY 12th 1859
AGED 80 YEARS
(RC-58)

PEACE AT ANY PRICE

Frances W. Pickens was the grandson of Revolutionary War Hero Andrew Pickens, and was actually born in 1805, despite what his headstone says. He was called a "Peace at Any Price Man" (similar to his epitaph). In part, because he was lukewarm on the idea of secession, unfortunately for him, he just happened to be Governor of South Carolina at the start of the Civil War.

Preventing the war proved impossible, and he lost many friends over his political stance and left office and unpopular governor. The war broke him and he lost a substantial portion of his wealth because of it.

IN MEMORIAM
FRANCIS W. PICKENS
BORN IN
ST. PAUL'S PARISH
APRIL 7th, 1807
DIED AT
EDGEWOOD,
JAN. 25th, 1869.

"MARK THE PERFECT MAN
AND BEHOLD THE UPRIGHT,
FOR THE END OF THAT MAN
IS PEACE."
(EF-2)

THOMAS WOODWARD THE REGULATOR

The Regulator movement (1765–1771) began in North and South Carolina just after the Cherokee War (1759-1761) and lasted until the Revolutionary War. Some historians believe it to be the catalyst of the American Revolution. Once peace was made with the Cherokees, it was hoped the lawlessness and raids along the frontier would end. In fact, raids and thievery increased by renegade Indians, armed bandits and runaway slaves. The British government offered little protection beyond the coastal cities and Colonial institutions, courthouses, and legal systems were corrupt and ineffective.

Colonist took matters into their own hands by forming Regulator groups to "regulate" the frontier, but British officials saw them as vigilantes and outlaws, sending out troops to put down the movement. By 1771, in South Carolina, the movement inspired acts by the British to protect colonists along the frontier and Regulators were eventually pardoned by the Colonial Governor. In the coming Revolution, Regulators like Thomas Woodward, rose up again to fight for American Liberty.

THOS. WOODWARD
THE REGULATOR
KILLED BY
BRITISH & TORIES
MAY 12, 1779
(FF-11)

THE "FRANK" OF SOUTH CAROLINA

Franklin (Frank) Elmore was one of the most powerful men in South Carolina during the years leading up to the Civil War. In 1839 he became president of the Bank of South Carolina, virtually controlling the political machine by controlling the money, and under him the bank became a tool used by State's Rights Democrats to dominate southern politics.

It could be said that the Bank of South Carolina was the Nation's first Super PAC. The Bank, under control by Elmore, was often charged with playing favorites, making politically motivated decisions and deceitful practices. Elmore's epitaph is a quote from Jesus in John 1:47. Ironically, it's sometimes translated as "Behold, an Israelite indeed, in whom there is no deceit."

FRANKLIN HARPER ELMORE
BORNE AT LAURENS S. C.
OCT. 15th ANNO DOMINI 1799
DIED AT WASHINGTON CITY D. C.
MAY 28th ANNO DOMINI 1850
"BEHOLD AN ISRAELITE INDEED,
IN WHOM THERE IS NO GUILE."
(RC-34)

THE CHRISTMAS FLOWER

Joel Poinsett was a Renaissance man. At first, he wanted to be a soldier, but his parents provided an education in law. Unhappy with a legal career, with decided to go on an extended tour of Europe and Russia. He made many political connections that would serve him later in life and learned many languages.

The well traveled Poinsett returned to the US where he was a Jeffersonian Republican and pro-Union. He was elected to SC State offices and became entwined in International politics and intrigue. Along the way he became a physician, a botanist and co-founder of the predecessor of the Smithsonian Institution.

Poinsett took great interest in South American politics, serving as a special agent in Chili and Argentina and later as the first minister to Mexico. While in Mexico he sent samples of the Aztec winter-blooming plant Cuitlaxochitl (*Euphorbia pulcherrima*) back home. It was soon known as the "poinsettia".

SACRED
TO THE MEMORY OF
JOEL R. POINSETT
WHO DEPARTED THIS LIFE
ON THE 12th DAY OF DECEMBER 1851
IN THE 73rd DAY OF HIS LIFE
A PURE PATRIOT AND AN HONEST MAN
AND A GOOD CHRISTIAN
(SM-4)

ROBERT SMALLS' BIG ADVENTURE

Born a slave, Robert Smalls with a crew of seven and their families escaped slavery by capturing the armed Confederate transport ship, the CSS Planter during the Civil War and delivered it to Union forces. The ship was filled with munitions and for his bravery he was made a captain and eventually given command of The Planter. After the war he returned to South Carolina and was elected Congressmen for five terms. His epitaph is a simple one and lies near a bust of Smalls celebrating his accomplishments.

ROBERT SMALLS
1829 – 1915
(BF-13)

PITCHFORK BEN

South Carolina's most "colorful" governor was "Pitchfork" Ben Tillman. Enlisting in the Confederate Army, but never serving because of loosing an eye, "Pitchfork" became a virulent racist. He established himself as a leading figure in the White Supremacy movement and as Governor (1890-1894), he demolished reconstruction and instituted the Jim Crow Era. As a US Senator (1894-1918) he was censured by the Senate and even barred from the Whitehouse.

However, Tillman had more dimension than his racist contemporaries. As a Populist, he championed the rights of the poor and farmers. He was key in establishing Clemson University and Winthrop University, as well as sponsoring the Tillman Act in 1907, the first Federal campaign finance reform law, banning corporate contributions.

Front Side:

BENJAMIN RYAN TILLMAN
BORN AUGUST 11, 1847 - DIED JULY 8, 1918
PATRIOT   STATESMAN
GOVERNOR OF SOUTH CAROLINA
1890 - 1894
UNITED STATES SENATOR
1895 - 1918
IN THE WORLD WAR-CHAIRMAN SENATE
COMMITTEE ON NAVAL AFFAIRS
A LIFE OF SERVICE AND ACHIEVEMENT

Left Side:

IN THE HOME
LOVING LOYAL
TO THE STATE
STEADFAST TRUE
FOR THE NATION
"THE COUNTRY BELONGS
TO US ALL AND WE ALL
BELONG TO IT, THE MEN
OF THE NORTH, SOUTH,
EAST AND WEST CARVED
IT OUT OF THE
WILDERNESS AND MADE
IT GREAT - LET US SHARE
IT WITH EACH OTHER,
THEN, AND CONSERVE
IT. GIVING IT THE
BEST THAT IS IN
US OF BRAIN AND
BRAWN AND HEART."

Right Side:

LOVING THEM HE WAS
THE FRIEND AND LEADER
OF THE COMMON PEOPLE.
HE TAUGHT THEM THEIR
POLITICAL POWER
AND MADE POSSIBLE FOR THE
EDUCATION OF THEIR
SONS AND DAUGHTERS
CLEMSON AGRICULTURAL COLLEGE
WINTHROP NORMAL AND
INDUSTRIAL COLLEGE.
(EF-10)

THE SWAMP FOX

The Legacy of Francis Marion, the "Swamp Fox" is massive. Arguably the greatest military mind and soldier South Carolina has ever produced, the father of guerrilla warfare, he and his men laid the foundation for the US Army Rangers. Marion experienced life at sea and was a veteran of the French and Indian War where he was to observe the fighting tactics of Native-Americans.

During the Revolutionary war under Horatio Gates, Marion was dismissed and sent out with his irregular militiamen, who like Marion, were citizen soldiers, fighting for their homes and using unconventional tactics. Always avoiding a frontal assault, the Swamp Fox, the name given to him by Col. Banastre Tarlton, proved to be a major nuisance to British forces by using guerrilla tactics and surprise attacks. Marion, both brutal and brilliant, was made Brigadier General and eventually joined forces with General Nathanael Greene to help bring a close to the war. The main character in Mel Gibson's film, The Patriot (2000) was largely based on Francis Marion.

SACRED TO THE MEMORY
OF
BRIG. GEN. FRANCES MARION
WHO DEPARTED THIS LIFE ON 27TH OF FEBRUARY 1795
IN THE SIXTY-THIRD YEAR OF HIS AGE
DEEPLY REGRETTED BY ALL HIS FELLOW-CITIZENS
HISTORY
WILL RECORD HIS WORTH AND RISING GENERATIONS
EMBALM
HIS MEMORY AS ONE OF THE MOST DISTINGUISHED
PATRIOTS AND HEROES OF THE AMERICAN
REVOLUTION
WHICH ELEVATED HIS NATIVE COUNTRY
TO HONOR AND INDEPENDENCE,
AND
SECURED HER THE BLESSINGS OF
LIBERTY AND PEACE.
THIS TRIBUTE OF VENERATION AND GRATITUDE IS
ERECTED
IN COMMEMORATION OF
THE NOBLE AND DISINTERESTED VIRTUES OF THE
CITIZEN;
AND THE GALLANT EXPLOITS OF THE
SOLDIER
WHO LIVED WITHOUT FEAR, AND DIED WITHOUT
REPROACH
(BK-5)

PRESTON S. BROOKS.
BORN IN EDGEFIELD VILLAGE.
AUGUST 6th 1819.
ELECTED TO THE STATE
LEGISLATURE IN 1844
ELECTED CAPT. OF COMPANY D,
PALMETTO REGIMENT, IN 1846,
AND SERVED DURING
THE MEXICAN WAR
ELECTED TO CONGRESS IN 1853,
AND DIED IN WASHINGTON CITY,
JANUARY 27th 1857.

PRESTON S. BROOKS WILL BE
LONG, LONG REMEMBERED;
AS ONE WHOM THE VIRTUES
LOVE TO DWELL,
THO' SAD TO US, AND DARK
THE DISPENSATION,
WE KNOW GOD'S WISDOM
ORDERS ALL THINGS WELL.
EVER ABLE, MANLY, JUST
AND HEROIC:
ILLUSTRATING TRUE PATRIOTISM
BY HIS DEVOTION TO HIS COUNTRY;
THE WHOLE SOUTH UNITES
WITH HIS BEREAVED FAMILY
IN DEPLORING HIS UNTIMELY END.
(EF-8)

*Few U.S. Congressmen are as notorious as Preston Brooks. Angered by a fiery abolitionist speech given by Senator Charles Sumner, Brooks severely beat Sumner on the head with a heavy walking cane. He required 3 years to recover from the injury.

WILLIAM BULL
OF SHELDON
BORN 1683, SON OF STEPHEN BULL,
THE IMMIGRANT.
MEMBER OF COLONIAL HOUSE OF COMMONS
1706 - 1719
COLONEL OF BERKELEY COUNTY REGIMENT
TUSCARORA AND YEMASSEE WARS.
LORD'S PROPRIETORS DEPUTY 1719
MEMBER AND PRESIDENT OF COUNCIL
1721 - 1737
ASSISTED IN LAYING OUT OF SAVANNAH
1733
LIEUTENANT GOVERNOR OF SOUTH CAROLINA
1737 - 1744
COMMISSIONER UNDER THE CHURCH ACT.
HE AND HIS YOUNGEST BROTHERS,
BURNABY AND JOHN BULL, WERE
COMMISSIONERS FOR THE BUILDING
OF SHELDON CHURCH
1753
DIED AT SHELDON, MARCH 21, 1755
HIS BODY LIES BURIED HERE.
(BF-13)

*ROGER MILLIKEN
"BUILDER"
(SP-5)

*Milliken's grandfather co-founded a small fabric company in New England in 1865, later acquiring property in Spartanburg, S.C. That site became the company's headquarters in the 1950's as Roger Milliken took the day to day operations. His epitaph is fitting since it was he who built Milliken & Company into a textile and manufacturing giant.

TOMB OF
ARTHUR MIDDLETON
1742 - 1787
SIGNER OF THE DECLARATION OF INDEPENDENCE
WHO IS BURIED HERE WITH

HIS MOTHER - MARY WILLIAMS -1721-1761
WIFE OF HENRY MIDDLETON
PRESIDENT OF THE FIRST CONTINENTAL CONGRESS

HIS SON - HENRY - 1770-1846
GOVERNOR OF SOUTH CAROLINA AND MINISTER TO
RUSSIA

HIS GRANDSON - WILLIAMS - 1809-1865
SIGNER OF THE ORDINANCE OF SECESSION

HIS GRANDDAUGHTER - ELIZABETH - 1749-1915
BY WHOM MIDDLETON PLACE WAS CONVEYED INTO
THE
CONTINUING CUSTODY OF DESCENDENTS OF
ITS ORIGINAL OWNER
(DC-1)

ON THE
18TH OF JULY ANNO DOMINI 1800
DEPARTED THIS LIFE
IN THE 61ST YEAR OF HIS AGE
*JOHN RUTLEDGE
J.R.
1800
(CT-26)

*First governor of South Carolina and a delegate to the
Constitutional Convention. He had a hand in writing the
U.S. Constitution and was the 2nd chief justice on the
Supreme Court.

*GEN. M. C. BUTLER
MAJ. GEN. C.S.A.
25th AUGUST 1864
1877-1895
18 YEARS IN THE SENATE
MAJ. GEN. IN U.S.A.
28th MAY 1898
PATRIOT, LAWYER, ORATOR,
SOLDIER, STATESMAN.
"KNIGHTLIEST OF THE KNIGHTLY RACE
THAT SINCE THE DAYS OF OLD
HAVE KEPT THE LAMP CHIVALRY
A LIGHT IN HEARTS OF GOLD."
(EF-3)

*Butler was an officer in the Civil War, loosing a foot to an artillery shell, returning to fight months later on crutches. A Southern Democrat, and active in State politics, he was elected as a US Senator. He played a role in the "Hamburg Massacre" launching the S.C. "Redemption" and the end of reconstruction.

HERE LIES
THE REMAINS
OF MAJ0R GENERAL
*MORDECAI GIST
AN OFFICER OF THE REVOLUTIONARY WAR.
HE DIED 12TH SEPTR. 1792
AGED 44.
(CT-27)

*Gist, originally from Baltimore Maryland, used a portion of his own wealth to raise his own infantry and was soon appointed as a brigadier general and his infantry division merged into the Continental Army. He retired in South Carolina and had two sons who he named "Independent Gist" and "States Rights Gist".

ANN PAMELA CUNINGHAM
BORN 15th AUGUST 1816 AND DIED 1st MAY 1875
AT ROSEMONT PLANTATION THE FAMILY HOME IN
LAURENS CO. S. C.
"IT IS GOOD FOR ME THAT I HAVE BEEN AFFLICTED"
"I SHALL BE SATISFIED WHEN I AWAKE WITH THY
LIKENESS"
THE FOUNDER AND FIRST REGENT OF THE
MOUNT VERNON LADIES ASSOCIATION OF THE UNION
1853   1874
BY HER EFFORTS AND IN RESPONSE TO HER APPEALS
THE PURCHASE MONEY WAS RAISED AND IN 1858
THE HOME AND TOMB OF WASHINGTON BECAME THE
PROPERTY OF THE MOUNT VERNON LADIES
ASSOCIATION OF THE UNION.
(RC-24)

*Ann Pamela Cunningham was best known for saving George Washington's home, Mt. Vernon, from neglect and decay.

MAXCY GREGG
BRIG. GEN. C.S.A.
MORTALLY WOUNDED AT THE
BATTLE OF FREDRICKSBURG, Va.
DEC. 13th, DIED DEC. 15th 1862 - AGED 47 YEARS
"IF I AM TO DIE NOW, I GIVE MY LIFE
CHEERFULLY FOR THE INDEPENDENCE
OF SOUTH CAROLINA."
"HE REST IN HOPE TO RISE."
(RC-17)

*Maxcy Gregg was an intellectual, a lawyer, political gadfly, and an authority on astronomy. Gregg threw himself into the Civil War effort. Though a "cultured gentleman," he was a fighting general who stood with his troops, ultimately costing him his life.

IN MEMORY
*LT. COL. WILLIAM WASHINGTON
BORN
STAFFORD CO. VIRGINIA
FEBRY, 28, 1752 - MCH. 6, 1810
LIVED IN CHARLESTON, SOUTH CAROLINA
AND HIS WIFE
JANE RILEY ELLIOTT
MCH 14, 1763 - DEC 14, 1830
FOUGHT AT LEXINGTON, CAPTAIN OF INFANTRY
AND WOUNDED AT BUNKER HILL
TRANSFERRED TO SOUTH CAROLINA AS
LT. COL. CALVARY
HIS TROOP FLAG PRESENTED TO HIM BY
JANE RILEY ELLIOTT
WAS BORNE IN VICTORY AT COWPENS
AND OTHER DECIDING BATTLES OF THE REVOLUTION
AND EARNED THE SOBRIQUET "TARLETON'S TERROR."
ON THE 52ND ANNIVERSARY BATTLE OF LEXINGTON
APRIL 19TH 1827 THIS FLAG
NOW CALLED THE EUTAW FLAG
WAS GIVEN BY HIS WIDOW
TO THE WASHINGTON LIGHT INFANTRY
OF CHARLESTON, S.C.
BY WHOM THIS STONE IS ERECTED
(CT-109)

*A Virginian and second cousin of George Washington, William Washington was on his way in becoming a clergyman before the American Revolution. With the outbreak of war, the young Washington laid down his bible and became a fierce warrior. As commander of the light dragoons under General Daniel Morgan, he helped turn the tide in the second half of the Southern Campaign. Washington was an equal match, if not superior to Col. Banastre Tarleton, his primary nemesis.

*GEN. WADE HAMPTON,
COLONEL IN THE REVOLUTIONARY WAR
MAJOR GENERAL IN THE WAR OF 1812
DIED IN COLUMBIA FEBRUARY 4th 1835
AGED 83 YEARS
(RC-50)

*Wade Hampton, Sr. was a competent soldier in the American Revolution and a less than successful General in the War of 1812. However, his real mark on history was in establishing his family as one of the most important in South Carolina history. On his death, he was the wealthiest planter in the United States.

SACRED
TO THE MEMORY OF
*WADE HAMPTON
1861 LIEUT. GENERAL C.S.A., 1865
SON OF WADE AND ANNE FITZSIMONS HAMPTON
BORN IN CHARLESTON
MARCH 28,1818
DIED IN COLUMBIA
APRIL 11, 1902
WHOLE HEARTED, TRUE HEARTED, FAITHFUL AND
LOYAL
THINE, O LORD IS THE GREATNESS AND THE
POWER AND THE GLORY AND THE VICTORY AND
THE MAJESTY; AND IN THINE HAND IT IS TO MAKE
GREAT AND TO GIVE STRENGTH.
1 CHRONICLES 29th CHAPTER 11th VERSE
(RC-51)

*Influential in South Carolina post-bellum history. A true outdoorsman and a natural soldier who was wounded five times during the Civil War. Sherman blamed Hampton's men for setting fire to surplus cotton bales as the reason for why Columbia was burned to the ground when he attacked the city.

UNDERNEATH
THIS STONE
ARE DEPOSITED
THE EARTHLY REMAINS OF
*CHARLES COTESWORTH
PINCKNEY
SON OF
CHARLES PINCKNEY
AND ELIZA LUCAS
BORN 25TH FEBRUARY 1746
DIED 16TH AUGUST 1825
(CT-20)

*Pinckney was a Revolutionary War hero and a Federalist in favor of a strong central government. He was a delegate to the Constitutional convention who advocated the idea that slaves should be counted as a state's basis for representation. He also believed that election by popular vote would be impractical and that US Senators should be men of wealth.

CHAPTER 11

CURIOUS CAPTIONS

"PARDON ME FOR NOT RISING"

..........THE EPITAPH OF HUMORIST DOROTHY PARKER

LILLIE RIPLEY
CONSORT OF
D. S. HENDERSON,
BORN
FEBRUARY 16th, 1856
MARRIED
DECEMBER 30th, 1876
DIED
FEBRUARY 17th, 1921

HER LIFE WAS AN OPEN BOOK
OF CHRISTIAN SERVICE.
SHE DIED IN THE FAITH-
A PEACEFUL DEATH

SHE IS A LILY OF THE
VALLEY UP YONDER
(AK-6)

SACRED
TO THE MEMORY OF
HUGH McLEAN
WHO DEPARTED THIS LIFE
THE 17th OF AUGUST 1821
AFTER A SHORT ILLNESS
AGED 25 YEARS

HIS DAYS WERE FEW HIS PLEASURES
LESS
BLAME NOT HIS HASTE TO HAPPYNESS
(KS-4)

J.W. EIDSON
BORN JAN. 28, 1842
DIED
JULY 11, 1906

GOD'S FINGER
TOUCHED HIM
AND HE SLEPT
(EF-9)

SACRED
TO THE MEMORY OF
ANDREW McKEE
WHO DEPARTED THIS
LIFE ON THE 13TH OF JULY 1800
AGED 51 YEARS

ALSO
TO THE MEMORY OF
JANE McKEE
CONSORT OF THE ABOVE
ANDREW
WHO DEPARTED THIS LIFE
ON THE 2ND OF DECEMBER 1820
AGED 70 YEARS

IN ONE GRAVE LIES THE
EARTHLY REMAINS OF
HUSBAND & WIFE
WHO HAD IN ISSUE, EIGHT
SONS AND TWO DAUGHTERS
(CS-1)

SACRED
TO THE
MEMORY OF
JOHN G. BROWN
WHO DEPARTED THIS LIFE
ON THE 14th OF
SEPTEMBER
1859
AGED 18 YEARS
AND 27 DAYS

MAN THAT IS BORN OF A WOMEN
IS OF FEW DAYS
AND FULL OF TROUBLE
HE COMETH FORTH LIKE A FLOWER
AND IS CUT DOWN
(RC-64)

*IN MEMORY
OF
WALSAMHAM GUNNELLS
(BUGGIE)
DIED SEPT. 26, 1923
AGE 65 YRS.
GONE TO HIS REWARD
(BB-2)

*On a Small Home-made Stone.

HERE LIES THE BODY
OF BIG O HENZY
WHO DEPARTED THIS
LIFE AUG.-28th-1787,
AGED 28 YEARS
(BF-7)

203

*IN
MEMORY
OF SISTER JANE
KIRPATRICK WHO
DEPARTED THIS LIFE
FEBR 29 1828, AGED 22
(CS-10)

*On a Small Home-made Stone.

UNDER THIS LIES THE BODY OF
MARY MIDDLETON
A PIOUS CHRISTIAN,
AN AFFECTIONATE WIFE,
A TENDER MOTHER,
A BEAUTIFUL DAUGHTER,
AND A SINCERE FRIEND.
WIFE OF THOMAS MIDDLETON
AND SECOND DAUGHTER OF
InO. BULL ESQR. AND MRS. MARY BULL
OF THIS PARISH

BUT
HOW LOV'D, HOW VALU'D ONCE, AVAILS THEE NOT.
TO WHOM ELATED, OR BY WHOM BEGOT.
A HEAP OF DUST REMAINS OF THEE.
TIS ALL, THOU ART, ALL THE PROUD SHALL BE.
SHE DIED FEBRUARY THE 2nd 1760
IN THE 37th YEAR OF HER AGE.
(BF-11)

GEORGE J. SIGWALD
DIED
NOVEMBER 16, 1891
AGED 37 YEARS

"GEORGE HAS GONE TO HIS HOME
FOR THE RACE IS RUN,
AND THE CROWN IS AROUND
HIS BROW,
THE ANGELS SAW WHEN THE
PRIZE WAS WON
AND THEY WILL LET HIM IN HEAVEN NOW"
(CT-97)

BENEATH THIS STONE
LIE THE REMAINS OF ANN DRAYTON
WHO DIED IN THE YEAR 1766

ALAS
ONLY THE 27th OF HER AGE
HER EXERCISE OF EVERY DOMESTICK CHORE
AS WIFE, AS MISTRESS, AS FRIEND
<u>SHE ASPIRED NO HIGHER</u>
CLAIMED THIS MONUMENT
OF
HIS CONJUGAL AFFECTION,
AND
GRIEF OF HER LOSS
FROM HER SURVIVING
HUSBAND
STEPHEN DRAYTON
(BF-12)

KATE ELIZABETH
WIFE OF
W. T. HALL
AND DAUGHTER OF
L. M. & M. C. BOSWELL
BORN IN CAMDEN, S. C.
DEC. 15, 1857
WHERE SHE DIED
NOV. 27, 1889
IN THE 32nd YEAR OF HER AGE
COME SEE YE THE PLACE WHERE I DO LIE,
AS YOU ARE NOW, SO WAS I,
AS I AM NOW, SO YOU WILL BE,
PREPARE FOR DEATH AND FOLLOW ME.
(KS-7)

HERE LYES THE BODY
OF MRS ELIZABETH NAIRN, WHO DYED THE 9TH OF
MARCH 1721, AGED 63 YEARS, SHE WAS MARRIED
FIRST
TO HENRY QUINTINE BY WHOM SHE HAD ONE SON
"HENRY"
WHO DYED IN THE SERVICE OF HIS COUNTRY
IN THE YEAR 1716 AND
TWO DAUGHTERS "MARY" AND "POSTHUMA"
HER SECOND HUSBAND, WAS THOMAS NAIRN,
JUDGE OF THE VICE ADMIRALTY OF THIS PROVINCE,
WHO WAS BARBAROUSLY MURDERED BY THE
INDIANS, WHILST HE WAS TREATING WITH THEM IN
THE YEAR 1715,
AND BY HIM SHE HAD ONE SON THOMAS

THROUGH MANY TRIBULATIONS
WE MUST ENTER INTO THE KINGDOME OF HEAVEN
(CT-18)

HERE
IN SILENCE LIES
THE DUST OF
MARY S. KENNEDY
WHO DIED ON 29TH AUG
1819
IN THE 21ST YEAR OF HER AGE

"MY DEAR YOUNG FEMALES,
THE DUST AWAITS
THE GLORIOUS CALL
TO JESUS"
(CS-12)

MRS. JANE WILSON
ROGERS
DIED JULY 30th 1803
AGED 25 YEARS

SARAH BROUGHT FORTH AN
ONLY SON
THEN BID THE WORLD ADIEU
THIS MOTHER HAD A TENDER
ONE
AND WENT TO GLORY TOO.
(FF-7)

JOSEPH E. GRADDICK
BLACK MALE
BORN 1-28-1943
DIED 2-6-1994
(GV-2)

SAMUEL C. HOLMAN
BORN
FEB. 14, 1866
DIED SEPT. 5, 1891

COME BACK, COME BACK
WE CANNOT GIVE THEE UP
IT IS HARD TO DRINK THIS
AWFUL DRAUGHT FROM
SORROWS BITTER CUP
(OB-3)

SACRED
TO THE MEMORY OF
WILLIAM H.
COMPTON
BORN MAY 6TH 1848
DIED NOV 8TH 1869
AGED 21 YEARS, 6 MONTHS
2 DAYS

CLOSE THEN MY SIGHTLESS
EYES
AND LAY ME DOWN TO
REST
AND CLASP MY COLD AND
DRY HAND
UPON MY LIFELESS
BREAST.
(CS-18)

SACRED
TO THE MEMORY OF
REV. JAMES FOY PETERSON
BORN
NEWBERRY CO. S.C.
OCTOBER 21, 1796,
DIED
IN EDGEFIELD CO. S.C.
JUNE 10, 1881
AGES 84 YEARS, 7 MONTHS
& 19 DAYS

"I KNOW THAT MY REDEEMER LIVETH,
AND THOUGH AFTER MY SKIN, WORMS
DESTROY THIS BODY, YET IN MY FLESH
SHALL SEE GOD."
(SL-1)

TO
THE MEMORY
OF
WILLIAM HERIOT
SON OF
ROBERT & MARIA E. HERIOTT
HE DEPARTED THIS LIFE
4TH JANUARY 1841
AGED 24 YEARS, 8 MONTHS
AND 16 DAYS
HOW SHORT THE RACE OUR FRIEND HAS RUN
CUT DOWN IN ALL HIS BLOOM
THE COURSE BUT YESTERDAY BEGUN
NOW FINISHED IN THE TOMB.
(CT-19)

TO THE MEMORY
OF
NEIL SMITH MERCHANT,
WHO DIED 17 AUGUST, AGED 35 YEARS:
AND OF
ISABELLA McLEHOSE,
HIS SPOUSE
WHO DIED 12 OCTOBER, AGED 32 YEARS:
BOTH AT CAMDEN IN MDCCCXXII.
THE FORMER A NATIVE OF BUTE. AND THE
LATTER OF GLASGOW: N.B. - HE WAS A DUTIFUL SON,
AND A KIND FRIEND. SHE ALSO POSSESSED
THE LIKE QUALIFICATIONS IN AN EMINENT DEGREE.
BUT SHE DID NOT REST HER HOPES OF SALVATION
ON THESE, NOR ANY OTHER HOWEVER EXCELLENT
IN THEMSELVES, NO, SHE TRUSTED ALONE IN THE
MERITS OF HER REDEEMER.

EPITAPH
IT MUST BE SO - OUR FATHER ADAM'S FALL,
AND DISOBEDIENCE BROUGHT THIS LOT ON ALL.
ALL DIE IN HIM - BUT HOPELESS SHOULD WE BE,
BLEST REVELATION WERE IT NOT FOR THEE.
HAIL, GLORIOUS GOSPEL ! HEAVENLY LIGHT,
WHEREBY,
WE LIVE WITH COMFORT, AND WITH COMFORT DIE;
AND VIEW BEYOND THIS GLORIOUS SCENE, THE TOMB,
A LIFE OF ENDLESS HAPPINESS TO COME.

ADMONITION
GENTLE READER, LEARN TO KNOW,
THIS WORLD'S A VAIN AND EMPTY SHOW;
THAT HEAVEN DESERVES YOU UTMOST CARE,
AND SACRED WRIT WILL GUIDE YOU THERE
(KS-15)

SACRED
TO THE MEMORY
OF
CATO ASH BECKETT
WHO DEPARTED THIS LIFE
ON THE 14TH OF JUNE 1851,
IN THE 61ST YEAR OF HIS AGE.
THIS IS ERECTED
BY AN OLDER BROTHER.
HE WAS A FATHER, TO THE
FATHERLESS, AND A HUSBAND,
TO THE WIDOW.
(CT-5)

CHARLES E. BAILEY
DIED APRIL 16, 1892
AGED 25 YEARS, 7 MOS.
AND 13 DAYS

IN THIS CASKET IN THE GRAVE YARD,
LIES A FORM THAT'S FAIR AND BRIGHT,
AND THE ANGELS GUARD HIS SLEEPING,
THROUGH THE DARKNESS OF THE NIGHT.
(CT-6)

OLIVER JAMES HART, JR.
BORN AUGUST 20, 1854
DIED JUNE 1, 1892
"UNTIL THE MORNING DAWN"

"I DREAMED NOT MY MOUTH
BECAUSE THOU DIDST IT."
(CT-8)

CAROLINE PINCKNEY
RUTLEDGE
1876 – 1952
"AWAKE AND SING
YE THAT DWELL IN THE DUST"
(CT-32)

UNDER THIS STONE INTERRD THE
REMAINS OF THE LATE GEORGE CUBHAM
OF LIVERPOOL MERCHANT WHO ON THE 29TH
OF DECBR 1784 EXCHANGED THIS TRANSI-
-TORY LIFE FOR A GLORIOUS IMMORTALITY

WITH SOUL SERENE HE KISSED THE CHASTING ROD
AND CHEERFULLY OBEYD THE SUMMONS OF HIS GOD
(CT-37)

SACRED
TO THE MEMORY OF
MARGARET BOYD
WHO DEPARTED THIS
LIFE FEBRUARY 17TH
1816 AGED 18 YEARS

DANGERS STAND THICK
THROUGH ALL THE GROUND
TO PUSH US TO THE TOMB,
AND FIERCE DISEASES
WAITS AROUND,
TO HURRY MORTALS HOME.
(CS-17)

AGNES JANE
WIFE OF
CAPT. JAS. P. MacFIE
BORN
DEC 15, 1835,
DIED
APRIL 1, 1883
O' DEATH, WHERE IS THY STING?
O' GRAVE, WHERE IS THY VICTORY?
(FF-4)

SACRED
TO THE
MEMORY OF
DOROTHY CONTY
WHO DIED JULY 27TH 1815
AGED 65 YEARS

WHEN THE DREAM OF LIFE
IS PAST, WHAT WILL IT ALL
AVAIL YOU IF YOU HAVE NO
TRACES OF UTILITY BEHIND
YOU?
(CS-19)

MARY L. CALDWELL
WIFE OF
R.B.CALDWELL
DIED JULY 24TH 1864
IN THE 38TH YEAR OF HER AGE
"THE SWEET REMEMBRANCE OF THE JUST,
SHALL FLOURISH WHEN THE SLEEP IN DUST."
(CS-5)

HERE LIES
THE BODY OF THE MUCH LAMENTED
REV WILLIAM RICHARDSON, M.A.
PASTOR OF WAXHAW CONGREGATION
FOR 12 YEARS AND RESTED FROM HIS LA-
BOURS ON THE 20TH DAY OF JULY,
A.D. 1771, AGED 42 YEARS

HE LIVED TO PURPOSE:
HE PREACH'D WITH FIDELITY:
HE PRAY'D FOR HIS PEOPLE:
AND BEING DEAD HE SPEAKS.

HE LEFT
TO THE AMOUNT OF
£340 STER'G
TO PURCHASE RELIGIOUS BOOKS FOR
THE POOR
(LC-8)

SACRED TO THE MEMORY
OF
MRS. EDITH MATHEWS,
DIED AUGUST 25, 1795
AGED 65 YEARS AND 10 MONTHS
OH! MAY MY LIFE BE LIKE MY PARENT'S BLEST,
MY MIND AS TRANQUIL AND MY SOUL AS PURE.
INCREASING FERVOUR SUPPLICATES THE REST,
A DEATH AS PLACID! A REWARD AS SURE
NOT FROM A STRANGER THIS HEARTFELT VERSE
THY CHILD INSCRIBES THY TOMB WHOSE TEARS
BEDEW'D THY HEARSE
(CT-24)

BARBARA CULP McKINNLEY
B 1733 IN PA,   D 1782 IN CHESTER CO.
DAUGHTER OF CASPER CULP
WIFE OF
WM McKINNEY B 1729 IN VA, D 1785
IN 1761 BARBARA SCALPED BY THE CHEROKEES
LIVED TO RAISE A FAMILY
(CS-21)

HERE
LYETH THE BODY OF
MARTHA BARNET
DEPARTED THIS LIF. IN THE
FIFTY THIRD YEAR OF HER AGE
SEPT'TH' 26 A.D. 1775
MY FRIENDS, THIS CLAY MUST BE YOUR BED
IN SPITE OF ALL YOUR TOW'RS
THE TALL THE WIFE THE REV'REND HEAD
MUST FLY AS LOW AS OURS
(LC-9)

LAURA POSTELL,
WIFE OF
DR. E. GEDDINGS
AND YOUNGEST DAUGHTER OF
EDWARD P. & SARAH
GIGNILLIAT POSTELL
DIED APRIL 2, 1879
"PEACE____
LET HER REST____
GOD KNOWS SHE'S THE BEST"
(CT-88)

SACRED
TO THE MEMORY OF
CAPT. MANUEL ANTONIO
WHO DEPARTED THIS LIFE
ON THE 12TH AUGUST 1796,
IN THE 57TH YEAR OF HIS AGE

ALTHO' I HERE AT ANCHOR BE,
WITH MANY OF OUR FLEET;
WE MUST SET SAIL ONE DAY AGAIN,
OUR SAVIOR CHRIST TO MEET
(CT-23)

NAPOLEON BONAPARTE
SON OF
WM. & S. C. RILEY
BORN
JUNE 2, 1859
DIED
JANY 8, 1885

YET AGAIN WE HOPE TO
MEET THERE,
WHEN THE DAY OF LIFE IS
FLED.
THEN IN HEAVEN WITH JOY
TO GREET THEE,
WHERE NO FAREWELL TEAR
IS SHED.
(OB-2)

IN
MEMORY OF
GEDEON JENNINGS ESQr.
AN AFFECTIONATE HUSBAND,
AN INDULGENT PARENT, AND
A FAITHFUL FRIEND;
HE DIED 11th FEBRUARY 1814
AGED 61 YEARS & 5 DAYS,
MUCH LAMENTED BY ALL HIS
FRIENDS & RELATIONS;
*BUT HIS BETTER PART YET LIVES
(OB-4)

Next to him lay his wife (his better part) who died a year later.

IN MEMORY
OF
MRS SARAH M. HORT
DAUGHTER OF W.H. VAUN, ESQ.
AND WIDOW OF ROBERT S. HORT, ESQ.
IN LIFE SHE IS KNOWN TO HER FRIENDS
AND IN DEATH
AS APPEARS BY HER LAST WILL
SHE LOVED HONORED AND SUCCORED
HER MOTHER THE CHURCH
LORD I HAVE LOVED
THE HABITATION OF THY HOUSE
AND PALACE
WHERE THINE HONOR DWELLETH
SHE DEPARTED THIS LIFE
THE 17 MARCH 1848
(CT-43)

SACRED
TO THE
MEMORY OF
SARAH BOYD
WHO DEPARTED THIS LIFE
MARCH 17TH 1824
AGED 66 YEARS

CORRUPTION, EARTH AND WORMS
SHALL BUT REFINE THIS FLESH,
TILL MY TRIUMPHANT SPIRIT COMES
TO PUT IT ON AFRESH
(CS-16)

SACRED
TO THE MEMORY OF
PAUL II A. MILTON
WHO BETWEEN THE YEARS
1732 & 1755
GAVE TO THIS CHURCH CERTAIN
SLAVES, TWO SILVER TANKARDS
FOR THE USE OF THE CONGREGATION
& £300.10

ALSO OF
JAMES L. ARDANT
WHO GAVE TO THIS CHURCH
CERTAIN SLAVES AND
£300
BETWEEN THE YEARS
1732 & 1755
(CT-1)

THE MORTAL REMAINS OF
DANIEL TOWNSEND
REPOSE BENEATH THIS STONE

AS A PARENT, HE WAS GENTLE AND AFFECTIONATE,
AS A HUSBAND, KIND AND MOST INDULGENT,
AND AS A MASTER, FORBEARING AND BENIGN,
AS A CITIZEN, HE WAS PATRIOTICK, PUBLICK
SPIRITED, AND PROMPT IN CONTRIBUTING
HIS FULL SHARE TOWARDS EVERY MEASURE
OF PUBLICK UTILITY
A FIRM WHIG; IN THE REVOLUTION OF '76
AND AT ALL TIMES, THROUGH LIFE, HE WAS TO BE
FOUND ON THE SIDE OF HIS COUNTRY.
AS A MEMBER OF SOCIETY, HE WAS COURTEOUS,
UNOBTRUSIVE, OBLIGING; AND AS A MEMBER
OF THIS CHURCH, AND A RULING ELDER, OVER THE
SAME,
HE ENDEAVOURED IN MEEKNESS, AND THE FEAR
OF GOD, TO DO HIS DUTY TOWARDS HIS BRETHREN.

HE WAS BORN ON THIS ISLAND (EDISTO), ON THE 17TH
DAY
OF JUNE 1759; AND AFTER RECEIVING FROM HIS
FELLOW CITIZENS, MANY MARKS OF THEIR
CONFIDENCE,
HIS INTEGRITY, AND PERSONAL VIRTUES;
AND AFTER PERFORMING WITH FIDELITY,
THE VARIOUS DUTIES BELONGING TO THE STATION
TO WHICH IT HAD PLEASED GOD [___] OF HIM HE
ON THE 21ST DAY OF_____

(CT-2)

219

IN
LOVING MEMORY
OF
ELIZABETH JANE LEE
"COUSIN JANE"
1850-1947
PROVIDED BY DISTANT KINSFOLK, AND
LOCAL FRIENDS THROUGH THEIR
PARISH SOCIETIES IN ST. JOHN'S CHURCH
IN WHICH SHE SERVED FOR 34 YEARS
(CT-75)

SICILY
HAMILTON
DIED
FEB. 12, 1923
AGED 52 YEARS
TIS HARD TO
BREAK THE
TENDER CORD
WHEN LOVE
HAS BOUND
THE HEARTS
(RC-21)

IN
MEMORY OF
JAMES S. WILSON
WHO DIED
JULY 24, 1849
IN THE 48 YEAR OF HIS AGE.

BY HIS SIDE LIES
LITTLE RICHARD.
(AB-3)

IN MEMORY
OF
NANNIE WITHERSPOON
THORNWELL,
DAUGHTER OF
REV. J. H. AND NANCY W. THORNWELL.
BORN JANUARY 16th A.D. 1839,
DIED JUNE 17th A.D. 1859,
AGED 20 YEARS,
5 MONTHS AND 1 DAY.
HER DEATH WAS TRIUMPHANT AND GLORIOUS.
SHE DESCENDED TO THE GRAVE ADORNED
AS A BRIDE TO MEET THE BRIDEGROOM.
(RC-19)

W.W. TRENHOLM
16, 1857

SEPT {

22, 1893
AND HE LED THEM FORTH
BY THE RIGHT WAY,
THAT THEY MIGHT GO TO A
CITY OF HABITATION
(CT-82)

ISABELLA DONALDSON
MARTIN
DAUGHTER OF
WILLIAM AND MARGARET MARTIN
BORN JUNE 24, 1839
DIED MARCH 4, 1913
AND THEY SHALL SEE HIS FACE: AND HIS
NAME SHALL BE IN THEIR FOREHEADS
(RC-66)

ON THE 24th JULY, 1859
WITH HEAVEN IN HIS EYE,
PARDON IN HIS HAND,
AND ANGELS FOR HIS
CONVOY,

THOMAS CRESWELL
BID ADIEU TO EARTH,
AGED 76 YEARS & 5 DAYS
(MC-8)

JOHN B. DAVIS
DIED
APRIL 30, 1885
AGED 28 YEARS, 6 MOS.
& 24 DAYS

THERE THE WICKED CEASE
FROM TROUBLING, AND THERE
THE WEARY BE AT REST.
(MC-10)

ESSIE LEE McCORD
WIFE OF
R. J. GILLELAND, SR.
AUG. 1, 1888
DEC. 20, 1955

THE MEASURE OF LIFE IS NOT ITS
DURATION, BUT ITS DONATION.
(AB-2)

*TO COMMEMORATE THE VIRTUES OF
ANN BEDDOWS.
A NATIVE OF YORKSHIRE, ENGLAND.
WHO DIED 11th NOVEMBER 1865.
AND IN GRATEFUL REMEMBRANCE OF
HER FIDELITY AND ATTACHMENT EVINCED
THROUGH VERY TRYING CIRCUMSTANCE
TOWARDS THE FAMILY OF
E. MOLYNEAUX Esqr. II.B.M.
CONSUL FOR THE STATE OF GEORGIA.
THIS MONUMENT IS ERECTED BY ONE
WHO KNEW HOW TO APPRECIATE HER
LIVING AND NOW MORNS HER DEAD.
(RC-49)

*This ornate (and costly) headstone is currently located within the sanctuary of Trinity Episcopal Church in Columbia, SC. Little is known about her, but local stories point to a love triangle that ended tragically.

SACRED
TO THE MEMORY OF
ELIZABETH FLOREN
OBT. APRIL 22ND 1798,
AGED 37 YEARS
HERE LIES A LOVING WIFE, A FAITHFUL FRIEND
A TENDER MOTHER TO THE END
HER SICKNESS SHE WITH PATIENCE BORE
PHYSICIANS WERE IN VAIN
'TILL GOD DID PLEASE TO GIVER HER EASE
AND DEATH DID CURE HER PAIN
(CT-51)

SACRED TO THE MEMORY
OF
MRS. HARRIET I. HOLME
DAUGHTER OF
Jo. ATKINSON OF CHARLESTON
AND SUCCEEDINGLY THE RELICT OF
DR. Jas. AIRAND I.L. HOLMES
OF THIS ISLAND
WHO CLOSED A LIFE OF SUFFERINGS ON THE
24TH OF NOV. 1829 AGED 18 YEARS

HAVING HER MISFORTUNES TO SUFFER MANY OF
THE ILLS CONSEQUENT UPON THE LOSS OF
RELATIVES AND PROPERTY
IT WAS HER MERIT TO GO THROUGH LIFE
FULFILLING CORRECTLY ITS VARIOUS DUTIES.
AS A MOTHER SHE WAS A BRIGHT EXAMPLE
AND NOBLY ENDURED FOR HER CHILDREN'S SAKE
ENOUGH TO BREAK THE STOUTEST HEARTS.
OF HER IT MAY BE SAID "WITH TRUTH."
(CT-11)

GEORGE
ELLA EUGENIA
1854
NOT DEAD
BUT GONE TO THAT SCHOOL
WHERE THEY NO LONGER
NEED OUR POOR PROTECTION
AND CHRIST HIMSELF,
DOTH RULE
(CT-12)

HERE LIES
THE BODY OF
ICHABOD BREWSTER
WHO DIED SEPT 11, 1814
AGED 29
READER: WOULDS'T THOU KNOW HIS FAITH?
CONSIDER THIS **T** EMBLEM **[A FEATHER]**
WOULDS'T THOU KNOW HIS LIFE?
ENQUIRE OF THOSE WHO KNEW HIM.
(CT-3)

SARAH JOHNSTON
BORN THIS PROVINCE
29TH MAY 1690
DIED 26TH MAY 1774
IN THE 84TH YEAR OF HER AGE
HOW LOVD HOW VALU'D ONCE AVAILS THEE NOT
TO WHOM RELATED OR BY WHOM BEGOT
A HEAP OF DUST ALONE REMAINS OF THEE.
(CT-29)

SACRED
TO THE MEMORY OF
CAPTN BENJAMIN MORGAN
WHO DIED OM THE
19 AUGUST, 1859
AGED
92 YEARS 8 MONTHS
WHO DESIGNATED HIS PLACE OF REST BY THE
INITIALS B.M. ON A TREE
(CT-69)

THE GRAVE
OF CATHERINE ADELA
CHAPMAN,
BORN 11 OCT. 1829
AND DIED
19 MAY 1848
AGED 18 YEARS, 7 MONTHS,
AND 8 DAYS
ELDEST DAUGHTER OF
JAMES AND ISABELLA
CHAPMAN

"ONLY AN EARTHLY PILLOW
TO BEAR MY DEATH-COLD HEAD,
AND THE TURF AND DROOPING WILLOW
TO DECK MY LOWLY BED."
(CT-64)

THIS
STONE IS ERECTED
IN MEMORY OF JONATHAN COOKE,
LONG A RESIDENT IN THIS CITY.
HE WAS A BENEVOLENT MAN, AN
AFFECTIONATE HUSBAND, BELOVED
BY ALL WHO KNEW HIM, AND MUCH
REGRETTED AT HIS DEATH.
HE DIED MAY 5TH 1796
AGED 79 YEARS

COME HITHER MORTAL, CAST AN EYE,
THEN GO THY WAY, PREPARE TO DIE.
HERE READ THY DOOM, FOR DIE THOU MUST,
ONE DAY LIKE ME BE TURNED TO DUST.
(CT-71)

HERE REST THE REMAINS
OF
HORATIO GATES
STREET
BORN 12TH NOV. 1777
DIED 31ST OCT. 1849

HAVING BEEN ALIKE
DISTINGUISHED FOR HIS
KNOWLEDGE AND ZEAL AND
FAITHFUL SERVICES
IN EVERY DEGREE OF
FREE MASONRY,
AND HAVING LIVED THE
LIFE OF A CHRISTIAN
HE LEFT US
IN THE FULL ASSURANCE
OF A SEAT IN THAT
GRAND LODGE ABOVE
WHERE THE SUPREME
ARCHITECT OF HEAVEN
AND EARTH PRESIDES.
(CT-4)

THOMAS W. DICKMAN
DIED DEC 18TH 1838
AE 20
NATIVE OF SPRINGFIELD, MASS
THOU DESTROYEST THE HOPE OF MAN
(CT-70)

MARGARET C.,
WIFE OF
THOMAS Q. ODOM.
AND DAUGHTER OF
JAS. E. & M.C. ODOM.
BORN NOV. 29, 1839,
DIED JULY. 16, 1887.

LORD, SHE WAS THINE,
AND NOT MY OWN,
THOU HAST NOT DONE ME WRONG.
(MB-1)

"BASS ANGLER SPORTSMAN SOCIETY"
GEORGE HUGHLAN RIVERS
HUSBAND OF EVA COTTRILL RIVERS
SEP 20 1925 - JULY 9 1988
(HM-12)

DETREVILLE FRANKLIN BOWERS
NOVEMBER 9, 1923 - DECMEBER13, 1991
"HIS LIFE MATTERED TO GOD. HIS DEATH GLORIFIED
JESUS CHRIST."
HUSBAND OF EVELYN PENDARVIS BOWERS
"HE TAUGHT US HOW TO LIVE AND HOW TO DIE"
CHILDREN
DETREVILLE FRANKLIN BOWERS, JR.
JOSEPH FORD BOWERS
PAUL RANSEY BOWERS
WILLIAM PENDARVIS BOWERS
"DADDY DIDN'T REAR SONS HE REARED BROTHERS"
EVELYN PENDARVIS BOWERS
(HM-13)

IN MEMORY OF RICHARD GOODING-
KNOWN AS "SQUIRE DICK"
DIED ABOUT 1839 AGE ABOUT 70 YEARS
SON OF JOHN GOODING,
REVOLUTIONARY SOLDIER
(HM-14)

And finally……The last Epitaph of this book……..

IN MEMORY OF
ROBERT LATTA
WHO DIED
AUGUST 25th 1852
AGED 69 YEARS & 4 DAYS
"VERSES ON TOMBSTONES ARE BUT IDLY SPENT,
THE LIVING CHARACTER'S THE MONUMENT."
(RC-28)

INDEX &

BIBLIOGRAPHY

COUNTY INDEX

ABBEVILLE -----AB

AIKEN ----- AK

ALLENDALE -----AL

ANDERSON -----AD

BAMBERG -----BB

BARNWELL -----BW

BEAUFORT ----- BF

BERKELEY ----- BK

CALHOUN -----CH

CHARLESTON -----CT

CHEROKEE -----CK

CHESTER -----CS

CHESTERFIELD -----CF

CLARENDON -----CD

COLLETON -----CL

DARLINGTON -----DG

DILLON -----DL

DORCHESTER -----DC

EDGEFIELD -----EF

FAIRFIELD -----FF

FLORENCE -----FL

GEORGETOWN -----GT

GREENVILLE -----GV

GREENWOOD -----GW

HAMPTON -----HM

HORRY -----HR

JASPER -----JP

KERSHAW -----KS

LANCASTER -----LC

LAURENS -----LR

LEE -----LE

LEXINGTON -----LX

MARION -----MR

MARLBORO -----MB

McCORMICK -----MC

NEWBERRY -----NB

OCONEE -----OC

ORANGEBURG -----OB

PICKENS -----PK

RICHLAND -----RC

SALUDA -----SL

SPARTANBURG -----SB

SUMTER -----SM

UNION -----UN

WILLIAMSBURG -----WB

YORK -----YK

SELECTED READINGS:

1. Combs, Diana Williams. Early Gravestone Art in Georgia and South Carolina. Athens, GA.: University of Georgia Press, 1986.

2. Curl, James Stevens. A Celebration of Death. New York: Charles Scribner & Sons, 1980.

3. E D Whaley, Mrs. Union County Cemeteries : Epitaphs of 18th and 19th Century Settlers in Union County, South Carolina and their Descendants. Greenville: A Press, 1976.

4. Edgar, Walter. South Carolina: A History. University of South Carolina Press, 1998.

5. Edgar, Walter, ed. The South Carolina Encyclopedia. University of South Carolina Press, 2006.

6. Gillon, Edmund V., Jr. Victorian Cemetery Art. New York: Dover Publications, Inc., 1972.

7. Graydon, Nell S. Tales of Columbia. Columbia, S.C.: The R.L. Bryan Company, 1981.

8. Helsley, Alexia Jones. Silent Cities, Cemeteries and Classrooms. Columbia, S.C.: South Carolina Department of Archives and History, 1997.

9. Maybank, Burnet R. (Sponsored by). South Carolina, a guide to the Palmetto State, compiled by Workers and Writers' Program of the Works Project Administration in the State of South Carolina. New York: Oxford University Press, 1941, Second Printing, 1942.

10. Rogers, George C., Jr. & Taylor, C. James (1994). A South Carolina Chronology, 1497–1992 (2nd ed.). Columbia, SC: University of South Carolina Press.

11. Wallace, David Duncan (1951). South Carolina: A Short History, 1520–1948.